Teaching Parents to Teach

Teaching Parents to Teach

A Guide for Working with
the Special Child

edited by

David L. Lillie and **Pascal L. Trohanis**
with **Kennith W. Goin**

Published by

Walker and Company
720 Fifth Avenue, New York, N.Y. 10019

for

Technical Assistance Development System
The University of North Carolina at Chapel Hill

Material in this book was developed with funds from a United States Office of Education Grant. Points of view or opinions expressed herein do not necessarily represent official Office of Education position or policy.

First published in the United States of America
in 1976 by the Walker Publishing Company, Inc.

Published simultaneously in Canada by Fitzhenry &
Whiteside, Limited, Toronto.

ISBN: 0-8027-0550-2

Library of Congress Catalog Card Number: 76-25732

Printed in the United States of America.

Book design by George Vornlocker

10 9 8 7 6 5 4 3 2 1

Foreword

After years of believing that the education of young children is primarily the responsibility of professionals in schools and other agencies, parents have begun to consider the potential for their own involvement in the training of their children. From community day-care centers to school kindergartens, mothers and fathers are seeking a more meaningful and participatory role in the lives and well-being of their children. Their aspirations are becoming a dominant and dramatic force in shaping the comprehensive care of the young in our society.

This book offers a framework for planning, organizing, and implementing parent involvement activities in early childhood programs. It brings together the knowledge and wisdom of professionals who have years of experience in working with parents and children. Most of the contributing authors are associated with the Handicapped Children's Early Education Program (HCEEP). This network of programs, funded by the Bureau of Education for the Handicapped in the U.S. Office of Education, is designed to demonstrate approaches for serving handicapped preschool children. The program has enjoyed enormous success in the six years of its existence, and it has shown great leadership in developing programs for parent involvement. While many of the thoughts and ideas presented in this text were born or nurtured in the HCEEP, we feel that they are in general applicable to parents and families of all young children.

The Technical Assistance Development System (TADS) was created to help HCEEP grantees achieve their goals by providing assistance in areas beyond the skills or fiscal resources available at the projects. In this capacity, TADS has had the opportunity of working with a wide range of talented people. We are pleased to have been instrumental in the development of *Teaching Parents to Teach*. We trust that it will be helpful and useful to many readers.

DAVID L. LILLIE
KENNITH W. GOIN
PASCAL L. TROHANIS

Acknowledgments

Many TADS's staff members have taken part in literature reviews, content and technical editing, designing, and typing materials at various stages in this manuscript's development. We would especially like to acknowledge the contributions of Susan Almon, Lee Cross, Rosemary Epting, Janet Grim, Sybil Jones, Helen Knight, Diane Leich, Jan Mandeville, Janet McCullough, Barbara Pearce, and David Wilson.

Contents

Teaching Parents to Teach

Part

An Introduction to Parent
Programs

An Overview to Parent Programs

David L. Lillie

Parent and family involvement is becoming more prominent in contemporary thought about child development and early education. All across the country, parents are engaging in activities that range from listening to lectures at parent meetings to making decisions about directions that child development programs should take. Because of this trend, professionals and parents are raising a number of crucial questions. Why the sudden rush to involve parents and families? Is a high level of parental involvement necessary for the success of a child-development program? Are parent-oriented programs to take the place of child-oriented programs? What is the relationship between the parent and professional? What approaches are most successful in working with parents? Unfortunately answers are not available for all of the questions. There is considerable information available, however, on parent and family programs for the development of young children, particularly young children with special needs.

One reputable pool of knowledge on programs for parents is the First Chance Network (funded by the Bureau of Education for the Handicapped in the U.S.O.E.). Officially known as the Handicapped Children's Early Education Program (HCEEP), this national Network represents a comprehensive attempt to demonstrate a number of educational approaches for young handicapped children. All of the demonstration programs (more than one hundred and fifty) in this Network have parent programs.

DAVID L. LILLIE is Project Director for the Technical Assistance Development System (TADS) at the University of North Carolina in Chapel Hill. His interests include planning for parent programs and child development.

3

The purpose of this book is to provide information that will assist the reader, whether parent or professional, in conceptualizing, planning, and implementing parent programs.

The Reasons for Parent Involvement

Perhaps the simplest argument for involving parents in child development efforts rests on the fact that during the early years of life, a large proportion of what the young, developing child learns will occur in the home. The parent, particularly the child's mother or mother surrogate, will be the primary "teacher." Her teaching style will be very important in shaping early motivation and cognitive functioning (Streissguth and Bee, 1972). Her role will not change even if the child is enrolled in a substitute care situation, such as a day-care center. It is not surprising that Gray (1970), Karnes, et al. (1970), and Levenstein (1970), among others, have argued that educational efforts in day-care centers, nurseries, Head Start centers, and public schools should be augmented with parent-training programs. After a review of research on the effects of parent-training programs, Schaefer (1972) concluded that such programs provide an effective supplement for or even an alternative to preschool education.

Unless there is planned consistency between the center's educational program and the experiences taking place in the home, the education provided at the center may have little effect on the child's development. Certain kinds of information that only the parent can provide about the child (such as how he is developing in the home) are needed in coordinating training between home and center. If parents relate their observations of the child's behavior in the home to center staff, more meaningful activities can be planned for both home and center.

The professional staff at the center can give parents the support they may need to work effectively with their child. Often, when parents recognize the existence of a problem or problems in their youngster, they focus exclusively on the negative issues, ignoring the more positive aspects of the child's behavior. Thus the normal aspects of the child's development may be overlooked. When parents notice that a child is having difficulty in accepting appropriate limits or discipline, for example, they may feel the youngster is not developing an adequate respect for authority and may become apprehensive about the possibility of serious consequences during adolescence and later life. They may not notice the times when the child's behavior is quite appropriate, or they may not respond to that behavior. In fact, they may be constantly on guard for misbehavior and may even set up artificial situations in which they attempt to exert authority. A child-development center's staff can encourage parents to foster an emotionally warm, secure relationship with their child, and to reinforce positive behavior.

There is another good reason for involving parents in child-development efforts. As consumers who are paying for the services, if not through fees then through public taxes, parents should participate in planning activities to assure that the type of services they want are the type of services they receive. The gap between parents' expectations and the services provided by the center or school must be narrowed through cooperation and coordination.

In most child-development programs, there is similarity between program and parent needs. Both are concerned with the optimal development of the child in all dimensions: physical, emotional, intellectual, and interpersonal. The program needs the parents' cooperation and assistance in a variety of ways: manpower assistance, program advocacy, decision-making, and cooperative planning for individual children. Parents, in turn, need support, advice, direction, and information from the program personnel. Goals for children will not be accomplished unless there is a close, compatible, multifaceted working relationship between the program staff and the family.

The Scope of Parent Programs: Four Dimensions

There are at least four major dimensions in planning parent programs that should be considered in a precise and systematic manner: supporting parents emotionally, exchanging information with parents, improving parent-child interactions, and getting parents to participate in the program. These dimensions are explored in the second part of this book.

Social and Emotional Support.   The purpose of activities in this area is two-fold: (1) to reduce the anxieties caused by guilt and feelings of inadequacy in the family and (2) to provide socially stimulating activities for parents which will increase the positive feelings they have about their family as a unit as well as about themselves as parents.

The birth of a child into a family is potentially a crisis. As parents strive to fulfill their roles successfully, many self-doubts often arise. Resentment of and confrontations with the child may become frequent. During crises, an educational staff can play a crucial role in supporting the parents both as individuals and as fathers and mothers.

The sincere teacher or child worker who listens carefully can give adequate support to most parents. A few parents, however, because of their emotional difficulties or lack of emotional support, may be overwhelmed by their feelings. Parents who find no relief in expressing their feelings to the staff of the educational center may need additional professional help.

Often the objective of social and emotional support programs for parents is to increase the parents' positive attitudes toward their role as educators of their children and, perhaps more important, to increase their feelings about their own importance as worthwhile human beings. Once identified, the social and emotional needs of parents can be met in many ways. Activities that revolve around a regularly scheduled meeting of a group of parents, for example, can provide a great deal of support. Topics in these meetings may vary from discussing various types of crafts that parents and children can do together to listening to book reviews or formal lectures from professionals. For the group meetings to be successful, it is important that members of the group indicate to one another through their actions as well as their words that these meetings hold value for them.

Exchanging Information.   Activities in this area should be designed: (1) to provide parents with an understanding of the rationale, objectives, and activities of the program in which their child is enrolled; (2) to develop the parents' understanding of the continuous growth and development of their child in the home; and (3) to provide educational personnel with background information—such as descriptions of the child's activities in the home—on the child, in order to increase the effectiveness of the center program.

There are many different kinds of information that can and should be given to parents about the program. Well-planned discussions or written information on what the center hopes to accomplish during the year are extremely important in maintaining parental support and interest. For example, parents should know what kinds of changes to expect in their child. When the educational goals have been articulated well, parents will understand the relationship and purpose of the many activities that go on during the year. Periodically, parents should be given a preview of their child's scheduled activities which includes an explanation of the activities' sequence and information on the expected results.

Routine information exchanges, between parents and the center's staff, are essential if information which is subject to frequent change, such as activity schedules, special events, parent conferences, and fee schedules (if fees are collected), is to be adequately brought to everyone's attention. Newsletters, form letters, and telephone calls are a few of the ways in which routine information can be handled.

Information about the home and the child are necessary for the sake of consistency between the center's methods and programs and those used in the home. For instance, information on what the child likes and dislikes, on the kinds of things that occupy his time at home, on the toys that are available in the home, on the relationship between brothers and sisters and the child can be invaluable to the educational staff in understanding the child's behavior at the center.

Many programs provide information to parents on child-rearing practices and child-development sequences. Often workshops are provided to assist parents in specific areas of child-rearing such as "teaching the child to talk" or "disciplining the child." This kind of information exchange is covered in what is referred to as "parent-child interaction."

Parent Participation.   The purpose of planning in this area is to involve parents in the ongoing activities of the program. By productively involving parents in various activities and roles, such as teacher's aide, the parents' feelings of self-worth will be enhanced. Their general understanding of children will increase, and they will have a larger repertoire of experience and activity from which to draw when interacting with their own child.

Parent participation in the program also provides some of the needed manpower for ongoing activities. Under the direction of the teacher or child worker, the parent aide can be involved in such activities as providing learning experiences for children, monitoring and assisting in lunches and snacks, assisting in removing and replacing heavy coats, constructing learning materials, and providing transportation. Usually, most groups of parents have some members with special skills, such as carpentry, baking, or storytelling. Other parents may have had interesting jobs or interesting experiences and can be resources for program activities.

Parents need to be involved in some of the basic program decision-making, perhaps as members of an advisory group. After all, the parent is one of the two primary consumers of the center's services. Since parents are involved in financing the programs through fees or taxes, moreover, it is reasonable that the program be accountable to them in program decisions. This is not to say that parents should unilaterally make program decisions. On the contrary, the program staff consists of trained professionals who provide several alternative approaches in most areas of the program. Parents should be able to look to and expect leadership from the staff in program decisions. In return, the center personnel should expect valuable assitance in program decision-making from parents.

Parent-Child Interactions. The fourth dimension of parent programs is training parents to become more effective "rearers" and teachers of their children. Through the years, the parent will be the child's primary source of information; consequently, he or she must be able to interact meaningfully with the child in order to stimulate cognitive, emotional, and social development. To facilitate parent-child interaction, an educational program should provide opportunities for parents to develop skills in (1) general child-rearing practices, (2) promoting and fostering social and emotional development, and (3) fostering and encouraging language and cognitive growth. Although perhaps an overgeneralization, most programs can be identified as following one of three models: *behavioral, psychological insight,* or *experiential.* The *behavioral* model employs a great deal of what we know about learning and development in a systematic, structured manner. In this approach, the parents are first taught some basic terminology and helped to understand reinforcement principles. They are also helped to develop the abilities of observing behavior and the frequency with which various actions of the child occur. After it is apparent that the parents have developed proficiency in observing behavior and counting frequency as well as in administering various types of positive reinforcers to the child, a long, formal relationship between program personnel and parent usually begins. At intervals, perhaps once a week, the parent reviews with a program specialist the results of his interactions with the child. By presenting and discussing behavior-frequency charts which the parent continuously uses, specific patterns of reinforcement become part of the parent's repertoire, and eventually the charting of behavior may be dropped.

A number of behavior-modification programs are available today. *Parents as Teachers: A Child Management Program* (1971) is designed to help parents learn to be more effective teachers of their children. *Living with Children* (1968) is another often-used book which details the manner in which parents teach their child. The parent-training approaches presented in this book have a strong behavioral foundation, even though they represent quite different approaches.

The *psychological insight* model deals with developing the parent's understanding of why children behave the way they do through an analysis of interactions between parent and child. This approach, which has been popularized during the last few years through the works of Haim Ginott (*Between Parent and Child*, 1959), emphasizes solving conflict situations by developing insight into the causes of the situations. Lectures and films on child development or personality development often are used to develop insight. Thomas Gordon's work in *Parent Effectiveness Training* (1970) is an example of a well-known psychological-insight approach.

Programs following the *experiential* model concentrate on providing parents with systematic experiences for optimal interaction with their child. These experiences may be focused either on an area of development, such as the case in *Teach Your Child to Talk* (1969), or on an age of development, such as presented in *Ways to Help Babies Grow and Learn* (1970). Each of these books offers suggestions for the parents in providing developmental experiences for their child.

Another recent development in helping parents provide positive interactions with and experiences for children is the toy-lending-library concept. After a discussion of the developmental level and needs of the child, the parent is given an appropriate educational toy to take home to the child. Usually instructions accompany the toy to give the parent an understanding of how it can be used for learning. Periodically, the parent will return the toy to the center and ask for another which is geared at a slightly higher level of developmental learning.

Parents as Resources (PAR), a group of parents in Illinois, has put together a series of suggested activities to increase the positive interactions between parent and child in the home. The group has developed two resource books for parents, *Recipes for Fun* (1970) and *I Saw a Purple Cow* (1972). These "recipes" provide many arts and crafts activities, which require articles already available in most homes, for parents and children to do together in the home.

The Operation of Parent Programs: Four Perspectives

There are four basic service-delivery systems described in the third part of this book: center-based, home-center based, home-based, and parent-administered center-based. These approaches represent basic organizational and managerial procedures for delivering the content of the program to the children.

Center-Based. The term "center" in this volume is broadly used as a label for any delivery system that brings children and parents into a central location. This central location could be a preschool classroom in a public school system or a clinical classroom in a university or private setting. In a center-based delivery system, the parent and family involvement program is often ancillary to the actual intervention activities with children, and the staff-parent interaction takes place almost entirely at the center. The desired result of these interactions, whether they are in the center or elsewhere, is a positive change in the child's or parents' behavior.

Home-Center Based. This service-delivery system is a combination of a home- and a center-based system, yet it requires organizational procedures different from those used in either the home- or the center-based approach. Parent-staff interactions in this approach take place both in the center and in the home. The interactions are sequential in nature and call for careful planning and coordination.

Home-Based. This system relies almost exclusively on providing educational intervention to the child through the parents. Since parent-child interactions in the home environment are the primary targets of intervention, much of the staff-parent interaction takes place in the home. Home-based programs do not provide for grouping children outside of the home for instruction as do center- or school-based programs. Consequently, there are a number of managerial dimensions that the staff needs to attend to that will vary from other types of delivery systems.

Parent-Implemented. In addition to the basic delivery systems, there have been some recent efforts to turn the entire management and operation of parent programs over to the parents themselves. This consumer-operated delivery system is yet another model, and it varies in a number of ways from the other three approaches.

Planning Parent Programs

In designing a program regardless of its dimensions or operational perspectives, it is important to follow a set of systematic procedures that allow all potential alternatives to be considered and a plan that clearly conveys the program's intent to be developed. Figure 1 presents four sequential steps that should be followed in planning efforts.

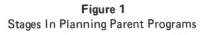

Figure 1
Stages In Planning Parent Programs

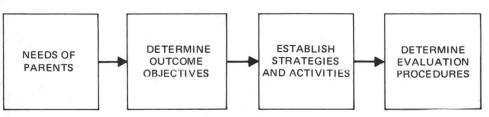

Determine Needs of Parents.   Before decisions can be made about what services and activities might be helpful to parents, it is necessary to determine what needs they have to function as parents, teachers, and individuals. These particular needs can best be uncovered if parents are involved with the staff in designing and executing the needs-assessment process. One method of conducting an assessment would involve building a series of open-ended questions which are based on the general questions listed in the "Needs" column in Figure 2. Specific questions, under each of these general questions, would comprise the content for an interview with each parent in the program. The information secured from the parents, which becomes the foundation for all subsequent steps in planning, should be organized in terms of the frequency and priority of various needs.

Determine Outcome Objectives.   Based on the needs of the parents, specific and precise statements about the outcomes that are expected to result from program efforts should be made. These statements should be phrased in terminology that makes it possible to determine if the objective has been successfully reached. An example of an objective in the area of emotional support is: *By the end of the project year, 75 percent of the parents in the program will demonstrate less anxiety about and more acceptance of their child.* An example in the area of information exchange is: *By the end of the*

Figure 2

Planning Parent Programs

PROGRAM AREAS	GOALS	OBJECTIVES	ACTIVITIES	EVALUATION
SOCIAL AND EMOTIONAL SUPPORT	What emotional support do parents need?	What changes do I want to occur by the end of the year?	What are the best ways to achieve those objectives?	How successful was I in meeting the objectives?
INFORMATION EXCHANGE	What information do the parents and center staff need from each other?	What information do I want known and by whom at the end of the year?	What are the best ways to provide that information?	How successful was I in meeting the objectives?
PARENT PARTICIPATION	What are the parents' needs to improve their interaction with their children?	What interaction and with what consistency do I want to occur by the end of the year?	What are the best ways to assure that these interactions take place?	How successful was I in meeting the objectives?
PARENT CHILD INTERACTION	What are the parents' and centers' needs for participation?	What participation is to take place by the end of the year?	What are the best ways to achieve the objectives?	How successful was I in meeting the objectives?

project year, the parents' knowledge of child-development milestones will be significantly increased over previous knowledge.

A mistake often made in planning is that too many objectives are established. If there are daily or weekly objectives for hundreds of areas, a major danger exists in becoming too engrossed in the objectives. Objectives should be used as a tool for planning; they must be kept in perspective; they are a means of getting the job done. One or two objectives written for each of the four parent-planning dimensions presented in this book should be entirely adequate for administering an efficient program. In some programs, depending on their nature, it may be unnecessary to have objectives in all of these four planning areas.

Establish Strategies and Activities.   Strategies refer to the sets of activities that are selected for use in reaching an objective. The questions listed under the "Activities" column in Figure 2 illustrate the need to plan activities very carefully, with objectives fully in mind. Many individuals begin planning by first considering activities, what they want to see occur day-by-day; this approach usually results in an ineffective program. The questions about needs and objectives, outlined in Figure 2, must first be answered. If a person doesn't know where he's going (objectives), how can he decide how to get there (activities)?

Determine Evaluation Procedures.   Evaluation involves determining whether or not objectives have been accomplished, by comparing objectives with the actual outcomes of the project. Many different evaluation procedures are available; standardized testing, criterion-referenced testing, observing and counting frequency of behaviors, and testimonials are some of the more popular.

It is essential to establish an evaluation method during the overall planning effort at the outset of the project. If evaluation is not considered at that time, it may happen that the objectives do not lend themselves to any type of evaluation, and it may be too late to change the plan effectively. Or, similarly, it may be found that the activities selected are ineffective in meeting the center's established objectives. This may have been avoided if the evaluation procedures were delineated before the activities actually started. Figure 3 presents a portion of a planning outline which deals with parent programs and demonstrates how each of the four planning steps can be placed into a concise and detailed plan. There are many good program-planning procedures available in the literature today.

Figure 3
Planning Outline

Target	Goal	Objectives	Activities	Evaluation Plan
Parents	Involvement of parents in partnership arrangements stressing the needs, strengths, concerns and special knowledge the parents have and utilizing the expertise of the professional.	To reduce anxiety by the end of the second year of the project in 90% of the parents.	Parent group discussion in which parents discuss their efforts to help their child on the problems they have encountered in such effort. A social worker will be assigned and will be available to each parent two hours a week for individual counseling.	Records will be kept listing parents who participate and their time of involvement. Anxiety levels will be measured by a scale (the IPAT 8 Parallel Form Anxiety Battery) as the parents enter the program and at the end of the second year.
		To increase in 80% of the parents an understanding of the programs' objectives and strategies for their children six months after their child is enrolled.	One week after the child is accepted into the program a family conference will be held at which time the program objectives and strategies will be explained. Written reports of the child's progress will be sent to parents monthly. Parents report the child's home progress to the staff in individual monthly conferences.	The Parent Program Evaluator will develop an instrument that will measure the parents' understanding of the strategies and objectives of their child's program. Each parent will respond to that instrument six months after their child enters the program either in writing or in a parent interview or both.
		To increase the effectiveness of the parents as teachers of their children using home-made toys.	Home Visitor visits child's home weekly to demonstrate to parents how simple toys can be made in the home. During the visits parents learn to utilize toys as learning tools.	An anecdotal record is kept of each Home Visit. Parent keeps a record of use of toys during the week. Video tapes of parent-child interaction are taped in the home weekly and critiqued by the Home Visitor and parent.
		To establish and implement three procedures that enable parents to give feedback to the project regarding their child's individual needs and the program in general.	A PARENT FEEDBACK BOX will be installed at the entrance to the center. The parent group will elect two parent representatives to the advisory council. Individual conferences between parents and staff will be scheduled monthly.	Parent coordinator checks PARENT FEEDBACK BOX weekly. Two parent representatives serve on the Advisory Board. A record is kept by Parent Coordinator of individual conferences between parents and staff.

The one discussed here is simple, straightforward, and has been used successfully by many new programs.

Programs for young children cannot afford to exclude parents from their procedures. Program staff members who are responsible for parent programs must operate within a well-defined framework as they systematically plan and operate programs for parents and children.

Bibliography

Becker, W. *Parents as Teachers: A Child Management Program.* Champaign: Research Press, 1971.

Cold, A., et al. *Recipes for Fun.* Winnetka, Illinois: Parents and Resources, 1970.

Cole, A., Hass, C., Bushell, F., & Weinberger, B. *I Saw a Purple Cow.* Winnetka, Illinois: Parents as Resources, 1972.

Enzer, N. "The Child-Development Triad: An Overview of Parent-Child and Professional Interaction." In D. Lillie (Ed.), *Parent Programs in Child Development Centers.* Chapel Hill, North Carolina: Technical Assistance Development System, 1972.

Ginott, H. *Between Parent and Child.* New York: Avon, 1969.

Gordon, T. *Parent Effectiveness Training: The "No-lose" Program for Raising Responsible Children.* New York: Peter H. Wyden, Inc., 1971.

Gray, S., Klaus, R., Miller, J. & Forrester, B. *Before First Grade.* New York: Teachers College Press, 1970.

Gray, S. & Klaus, R. "The Early Training Program: A Seventh Year." *Child Development,* 1970, 41, 909–924.

Karnes, M., et al. *Goal: Language Development.* Springfield, Massachusetts: Milton Bradley, 1972.

Levenstein, P. "Cognitive Growth in Preschoolers Through Verbal Interaction with Mothers." *American Journal of Orthopsychiatry,* 1970, 40, 426–32.

Patterson, G. R., & Gullion, M. E. *Living with Children: New Methods for Parents and Teachers.* Champaign: Research Press, 1968.

Pushaw, D., Collins, N., Czuchna, G., Gill, G., O'Betts, G., & Stahl, M. *Teach Your Child to Talk.* Cincinnati: CEBCO Standard Publishing Company, 1969.

Schaefer, E. "Parent as Educators: Evidence from Cross-Sectional, Longitudinal, and Intervention Research." In W. W. Hartup (Ed.), *The Young Child.* Washington: National Association for the Education of Young Children, 1972.

Segner, L. & Patterson, C. *Way to Help Babies Grow and Learn: Activities for Infant Education.* Denver: World Press, 1970.

Streissguth, A. P., & Bee, H. C. Mother-Child Interactions and Cognitive Development in Children. In W. W. Hartup (Ed.), *The Young Child* (Vol. 2). Washington: National Association for the Education of Young Children, 1972.

Parent-Child and Professional Interaction

Norbert Enzer

Parents, and occasionally others in the family, must interact with those who operate programs for children. Whether we address ourselves to day care for the very young, early education, or intervention programs for children with special needs, parental involvement must complement professional efforts with the child. If a program has goals for progressive development or change rather than simply time-filling activity for both child and staff, those responsible have the obligation of clarifying those goals to parents and gaining their assent. Only then will professionals have the opportunity of enlisting parents as invaluable allies.

Agreeing on Goals

Parents do influence a child's activities, interests, and his willingness to participate. In 1931 Pearson concluded that "parental attitudes exert a more important influence on the formation of the child's personality than the actual events." Freeberg and Payne (1967) quote a number of studies indicating the importance of parental attitudes on their child's intellectual achievement and motivation. The parent who, by word and deed, expresses an investment in learning and a genuine and benevolent interest in his child's acquisition of skill and knowledge is likely to see joy and achievement

NORBERT B. ENZER is Chairman of the Psychiatry Department at Michigan State University in East Lansing. His publications and presentations reflect his interest in families, child development, and the handicapping conditions of childhood.

in school. On the other hand, those parents who for whatever reason convey a distrust of the school and its teachers, a disrespect for or a disinterest in education, and attitudes of "look at me, I never finished grade school" or "it's not what you know but who," often find a similar disinterest in their children, whose academic performance is frequently poor.

In point of fact, it is virtually essential that there be a commonality of goals between a child's family and those professionals who work with a child outside his family. One aim of work with parents is clearly to insure that there is agreement about goals. This may seem an obvious point, but what is said aloud may not be what is meant. Those who work with children are familiar with the situation in which a young child's progress toward independence and self-assurance is hindered or stifled by a parent's overly fearful concern for safety. Though parents in such situations may well express a desire for autonomy in their child, their behavior and their attitudes are influenced by other factors.

Such a situation often arises when there is unconscious hostility toward the child, dating to very early infancy or even to prenatal life. Such hostility results in feelings of guilt, and unconsciously the parent often attempts to compensate by overtly being a superlative guardian. He tries to keep the child close, and he does (rather, overdoes) for the child to compensate for hostility and guilt. In this way, he presents a public image of a "good parent." But from the child's view, such interaction of emotions and behavior creates smothering mothers and appeasing fathers. Though this is not an uncommon pattern in the general population, it is a particularly frequent occurrence in the families of children with handicapping conditions. Feelings of rejection may be compounded by disappointment, and guilt may be magnified by a sense that the parents themselves are responsible in some way for the handicap or defect.

This psychological phenomenon demonstrates that the parents who may consciously and verbally agree that a goal is appropriate may deep down reject it, in part because the opposite situation satisfies some of the parents' needs. Parents' internal needs and feelings can interfere with progress and can actually undermine therapeutic programs, even though the parents express agreement and consent.

Establishing a Parent and Professional Alliance

It is essential that a true alliance be created with the parents. Fundamental to such a relationship is mutual respect, honesty, and an egalitarian attitude on the parts of both workers and parents. While occasionally parents do present themselves with these assets, it is more likely that the climate will have to be created. No one can produce such an atmosphere unless he or she is willing from the outset to be nonjudgmental of parents, to understand that there are needs and feelings of which the parents themselves may be unaware and that, though parents may have little formal knowledge of child development or of parenting, they have a great deal to offer, and all can learn.

Parents may approach a helping situation with widely differing attitudes. They may believe that they have little to contribute and are helpless. They may look to "experts" for direction and full responsibility, or they may view all helpers with suspicion and anger. Parents who present themselves as being inadequate may be seeking advice and guidance or they may be testing the resourcefulness of the helper. Focusing on some particularly appropriate interaction with their child and commenting, "you seemed to sense his needs very well" or "you seem to be saying that he enjoys it when you do that and you sound as if you do too" or simply "that sounds good," may be very supportive and helpful.

When parents are hostile or skeptical, it is better to bring their feelings into the open rather than attempt to placate them. Often parents of children with chronic illnesses or handicaps have been frustrated and disappointed by others. If the professional recognizes these feelings by saying something, like "that must have been disappointing," when the parents recall their anger about the lack of help elsewhere, it may help parents relate their feelings. This gesture conveys to them that the helper is willing to listen to the frustrations of the past. Allowing parents to give a complete history in their own way and at their own pace and giving them specific opportunities to present some of their child's assets will help to convince the parents that the worker is really interested in their opinions, ideas, and observations. All parents have concerns for and problems with their children, but this is especially true of parents of children with some handicap or chronic disturbance.

One must never take concerns lightly. They are always serious to parents or they probably would not be mentioned, though there may be even more important worries that the parents will convey once they have assured themselves the helper will listen. It is not an uncommon occurrence for a mother and child to be in the family physician's office for a school checkup or some minor complaint and at the end of the examination the mother says in an offhand manner, "Oh, by the way, Doctor, Suzie has been very sassy lately." In many cases, it is apparent that the real reason for the visit was not the initial complaint about a minor physical symptom, but rather the concern the mother was hesitant to present. In this illustration, if the physician brushed aside the mother's initial complaint or did not seem to listen to her, the second more important concern might not have emerged. Saying "I would not worry about that" is rarely helpful. "I can see you are concerned" or "you must have been very worried" is much more likely to offer parents the encouragement they need to say more. Furthermore, judgments about the seriousness of parental concerns are never justified until there is a good deal of information available upon which to make such a judgment.

So much depends on the quality of the initial contact with the parents that it is frequently most helpful to use the initial visit simply to "set the stage." For example, a psychiatric consultation was requested for a young boy hospitalized to investigate rather long-standing, but vague, complaints. Nothing had been found in initial studies, and it was considered likely that the symptoms resulted from emotional or interpersonal conflicts.

The psychiatrist found the mother resentful that such a possibility was considered. She believed it somehow implied there was "nothing physically wrong" and that she was at fault for the problem. The consultant elected to listen to these feelings and to the mother's very great concern and fears during his first visit. Following this, the mother related more positively and offered a detailed history which had not previously been obtained that provided the basis for specific tests, the results of which did establish a diagnosis of an early form of a serious but treatable chronic illness. In this case, the mother provided historical information about her son's illness to the psychiatrist that she had not offered to others. She said that others were too busy to ask for details. She further indicated that she was often so upset in previous interviews with others that she would become "mixed-up" or forget things.

Reliable information exchange requires a relationship of mutual trust and respect. Parents are not likely to offer maximum information without a solid relationship, and they are certainly not likely to accept professional opinions or suggestions unless they trust the person making the suggestions. All too many professionals hide behind their degrees and pontificate wisdom to parents without the slightest recognition of interpersonal factors. This unfortunate situation, along with the nature of the information and the language, often accounts for the fact that so many families seem confused and disappointed, and so many do not follow the advice that is given.

People do not listen well if they are upset by a situation. It is often remarkable how much can be accomplished by patient, thoughtful, and empathic efforts to improve the communication pattern between parents and helpers.

Matheny and Vernick (1969) have demonstrated the effect that improving parent-staff communications has on parental attitude. In their study, they promised to discuss "everything" with parents, and they encouraged parents to participate in the evaluation of their child and to ask questions. It was suggested to the parents that they should not hesitate to put pressure on the staff to communicate, and if there were difficulties or further questions a particular staff person was available to help manage or interpret communication problems. Though relatively little time was devoted to these efforts, most parents did show significant positive change in their expectations for and behavior with their retarded child.

It is of utmost importance in the creation of an alliance, that the parents believe those offering help can in fact be helpful. Professionals must demonstrate respect for and honesty with parents, as well as display competence.

Recognizing Assets in Children

The interactions between parent and child must be as productive and adaptable as possible. Parents must be encouraged to develop an emotionally warm, secure relationship with their child and to support and reinforce progress and positive behavior. Very often, parents tend to focus on problems and ignore the more positive aspects of the child's functioning and behavior or to minimize other important aspects of his life. For instance, when parents note that the child is having difficulty in accepting appropriate limits or discipline, they may feel the youngster is not developing an adequate respect for authority, and may become apprehensive about serious consequences that such behavior may have during adolescence and later life. They may not notice the times when the child's behavior is quite appropriate or they may not respond to that behavior. In fact, they may be constantly on guard for misbehavior and may even set up artificial situations in which they attempt to exert authority.

In one such case, a mother decided that her little first grade daughter should wear certain clothes to school each day. The effect of this decision was that each morning there was a lengthy, angry, often tearful interaction between mother and daughter, at times end-ing with the mother's acquiescence to prevent tardiness. Though this interaction was totally negative in content, the daughter did get her mother's undivided attention. When this quality was discussed with the mother, she recognized that the issue of dress was really quite trivial; and that she was so concerned about what she viewed as the beginning of a serious behavior disorder that she felt she had to "pick up" on any and all rejection of her authority.

While both parents gave numerous examples of problems, some of which were of greater consequence than the dress incident, they had trouble recounting specific examples of positive behavior, though both admitted that the child was not "bad all the time." They did come to recognize that they, in fact, were ignoring her more appropriate behavior and were instead responding primarily to the inappropriate. They really were missing the joy and satisfactions of their daughter's achievements, and she, on the other hand, was performing in a way that brought a predictable, but negative, response. In a sense, the little girl was substituting parental attention (negative attention) for parental approval.

Social interaction, even negative interaction with people who are important in our lives, can be reinforcing, and it is often better to be scolded than to be ignored. On both sides there was anger and disappointment. The parents felt the little girl was deliberately trying to antagonize, and she felt unloved and unappreciated. In this case, much was accomplished as the parents began to interact with the child in an appropriate manner, to ignore the trivial, and to discipline fairly and with a minimum of interaction. Perhaps equally significant were the profound changes in the emotional relationship and the pleasure the parents experienced in their daughter's success; she in turn began to feel increased self-esteem.

A clear recognition of assets is of great value for parents and for others involved with children. Knowledge about a child's strengths, interests, and play can be used by teachers, therapists and others in motivating and establishing rapport with the child. Furthermore, such attention conveys to the parents the staff's interest in the totality of the child's life, not just in some dimension of pathology or deviance. Frequently parents who ask for help are so worried and anxious about their child that their own view is distorted. They need to develop some balance in their assessment of the situation. Parents of handicapped or disturbed children often need help to see the joy and satisfaction of being parents.

A discussion of assets often makes parental attempts to deny certain aspects of the problem seem very obvious, which is helpful to parents in recognizing that they have been trying to hide things from themselves.

Communicating with Children

In the presence of developmental disturbances in the child, communication problems can often seriously complicate interactional and emotional difficulties. Attempting to interpret the immediate needs and demands of a young child are difficult enough for any parent, but when there are disturbances in perception—particularly auditory perception—or disturbances or delays in verbal communication and language, misinterpretation may become critical.

The young child tends to interpret literally what is said to him. It is worth noting that to the three-year-old there really is quite a difference between being told "you are a bad boy" and hearing "it is bad to kick the cat." If there is a delay in cognitive development, the usual development of more symbolic language is delayed; concrete, literal interpretation consequently continues. Related to the difficulties that arise because the young child cannot appreciate symbolic communication are the problems caused by destructive or incendiary communication. When anger or frustration is expressed toward the child, it often tends to be personally denigrating. "You are a careless slob" is a comment that conveys disappointment and rage. It is "attacking" and abusive and is likely to inflame. It does not allow a productive response. On the other hand, "It really gets my goat when you don't clean your room" carries a clear explanation of the unacceptable act and focuses on the behavior, or lack of it, rather than on the person. It is a sufficiently clear statement about the offense that the child has some idea of the expected response.

Questions also can pose problems in communication with young children and with those delayed in cognitive development. As adults we often find it more appropriate to request rather than command. More often than not, adults recognize the difference between a true question and a rhetorical question for which compliance is expected. To say "Will you please come to the table?" may be quite appropriate with adult guests at a dinner party. A similar question to the young child may be answered with a "no," for he may well view it as a question rather than a request for action. "Will you clean up your room?" may be ignored, while "Clean up your room!" may produce a fairly prompt response. Parents can often gain considerable insight into the child's logic if, with the help of a parent worker, they attempt to place themselves in the child's place and try to imagine how he might react.

Understanding Behavior and Self-Control

Human beings are not born with self-control; they develop it only gradually in a manner more or less concomitant with early cognitive development. For practical purposes, it may be said that in the first year of life there is no self-control. After that time, controls develop gradually.

Initially, the control of behavior is acutely related to specific people, places, and times. The little child may not touch his mother's favorite ashtray in the living room if she is present. But if she is not, he might. If mother reprimands him for touching the ashtray but father does not, the child is left confused about ashtrays. He may "behave" in mother's presence but not learn to generalize to other ashtrays in other rooms.

These primitive controls are largely related to the anticipation of some negative response from others or to a past experience of pain or injury. It is not until about the time when he enters school that the average child develops an internal sense of something being "wrong." Often parental concern about mischievous or negative behavior results because the parents do not appreciate the fact that the young child has not developed a *real* capacity for self-control. Too much is expected.

Expanding the Role of Parents

Attempting to improve the quality of parent-child interactions may be very useful in extending intervention efforts. Particularly in those situations where there are specific therapeutic or habilitative efforts for disabilities, however, it is essential that parents actually learn more about the nature of the disturbance and the specific techniques which are useful in dealing with it. This may mean providing parents with the skills needed to use certain procedures in the home. Care must be taken by professionals to define the boundaries and limitations of this type of effort because parents may focus so completely on certain technical and highly specific procedures that they may ignore other aspects of the child's life and of their interaction with him.

A similar word of caution can be expressed to all who work

with exceptional children. Many people in programs for children with learning disabilities, for example, devote so much time and effort to the remediation and development of specific educational skills that they forget that there is a need to teach general information as well. The child with dyslexia may not be able to acquire information from the printed page, but he can often acquire it through auditory means. His need to know about the world and its people is no less than the child who reads well. The role of teacher or therapist may complicate the role of parent. It is critical that both parents and program personnel continue to recognize the primacy of the parental role and its essential place in the child's development. Parents can work with their children, but they must continue to be parents.

Helping the Whole Family: A Need for Balance

Another aim of parent work is strengthening or stabilizing the general family situation. It is generally accepted that the home in which there is emotional warmth, mutual respect, encouragement, the opportunity for communication, honesty, consistency and security is the optimal setting for the child's development. Achievement of such qualities in a home may be beneficial for any child. Some parents may well need help in working toward that goal.

The family with a handicapped, deviant, or chronically ill child has special problems which set the stage for unique pitfalls. Pediatricians are all too familiar with families of children who have serious chronic or life-threatening illnesses. The devotion of economic resources, emotional and physical energy, as well as time itself, to one member of the family may produce a situation in which others suffer needlessly. Such a danger exists even when parents are truly involved in trying to aid any child in the family who has a problem. All of us have seen the mother of a retarded child devote so much to that child that she offers little to the others in the family.

There is no denying that children with special problems need special help. However, it is essential that professionals involved with these families recognize the need for balance, and that they constantly remind themselves and the parents that others have needs as well as the special child. Too often an exceptional child is a seed which, if nourished inappropriately, can become a destructive weed within the family. The guilt, anger, and disappointment within the parents can be magnified and displaced. The devotion to the one child can be rationalized because of the child's needs, and the feelings and needs of others can be denied for the same reasons. It would seem that even the most skillful therapist might have great difficulty in managing some situations. However, in many situations families can be aided in avoiding the tragic problems which naturally impede the progress of the child whose problem seems to be the axis about which all of this disruption occurs.

An alliance with parents offers a foundation for strengthening a family. Some have found that with appropriate direction and assistance—which often means providing nothing more than a sounding board for family emotions—families can become closer and stronger. It is worth mentioning, in passing, that certain cases do arise in which stability may only occur with the separation or divorce of parents. If the parents believe they cannot continue to live together in harmony and are only staying together because of the guilt or other feelings centered on the presence of a handicapped child, the reality of these feelings must be explored. It is often most difficult for parents to recognize their own feelings and needs in the presence of a child with problems, and it is particularly difficult for some parents to separate themselves from an intolerable union if it would appear to others that they were deserting a handicapped child.

Parent as Volunteer Worker

A final goal of parent programs is that of enlisting the aid of parents in various aspects of programmatic work and/or support. We have seen abundant examples of the effectiveness of parents in aiding the creation of child development programs, in supporting and sustaining programs, in providing public information and in creating public interest.

Preparing for Progress

There are times when, because of the severe nature of a child's problem or because of a disruptive or noxious influence within the home, it is appropriate for a child to be removed partially or totally, at least for a time, from his family.

Children can change, and even the most handicapped may progress. Parents and families may need considerable help in adapting to change. The changes that occur in a child require new or alternative behavioral responses on the part of parents. While this is true with remediation of all handicaps, it is especially true if a child has been out of the home.

For example, one little retarded boy was sent to a special residential school at about age seven. For all practical purposes, he had no self-help skills, and the family seemed quite overwhelmed by this and other problems. While he was away, help was offered to the family, but they refused it. At the end of a nine-month stay at the school, he was returned home with the ability to dress and feed himself. He was much more facile in making his needs known.

Initially, the family saw him as demanding, stubborn, and selfish. The mother continued to try to dress and feed him for she could not believe he could do either correctly. Within a few months, gains had largely been lost and there was, in addition, punitive parental behavior in response to what the parents saw as a behavior disturbance. The original equilibrium, which had been troublesome to the parents and not conducive to change in the child, had been altered, and no preparation had been made for the reentry of the child into the family and for parental adaptation to the progress he had made.

Clearly, children need their parents. They have basic biological needs which are usually the responsibility of parents, but they need much more. Every child needs emotional warmth and security, a feeling that others respect and value him, a recognition that those adults most important to him appreciate his achievements and his accomplishments. Each child needs a sense of belonging, a focus for his own emotions, benevolent controls, discipline, a concern for his safety, and role models.

Parents have needs too—needs which can only be fulfilled by their children. They need to feel the responsive warmth of love in return for their attention to the child. Few parents seem as sad as those of the unresponsive infant, who doesn't seem to care about the presence or absence of parental attention. They also need to feel that they are "good parents" and that their child is progressing toward the goal of health and happiness. They need to feel a sense of pride in their offspring.

For some parents, the emotional investment in their child is clearly excessive and pathologic. They may have expectations beyond the child's capacities, or they may want to live vicariously through the child. It is these parents who are most vulnerable to the impact of a handicapped youngster. The feelings of guilt, anger, rejection, disappointment, and stigma which are present to some degree in all parents of developmentally disabled children can have particular impact on those parents who tend to invest excessively in their children. In all cases, it is part of the task of the parent worker to aid in bringing about a balance between the child's needs for his parents, the parents' needs for their child, the needs of the parent partners for each other, and the needs of others in the family.

Similarly, there are common needs between the child-development staff and the parents. Both are concerned with the optimal development of the child in all spheres—physical, emotional, intellectual, social, and interpersonal. Both hope the child will reach the highest possible level of adaptation. The program staff needs the parents' cooperation and assistance in a variety of ways, as will be documented in subsequent chapters of this book. The parents need support, advice, direction, and information from program personnel. None of this can be accomplished, and the child's progress will suffer, unless there is a close, compatible, working relationship between the program staff and the family.

The presence of a handicapped or exceptional child places a very special kind of stress on the integrity of a family and its individual members. Though specifically concerned with parents of a mentally retarded child, the Group for the Advancement of Psychiatry outlined some factors applicable to other handicapping conditions.

> The physician is dealing with parents who have a multifaceted problem: I. They may not have fully accepted the diagnosis of mental retardation. II. They have varying degrees of guilt feelings about their possible role and about the causation of the child's condition. III. They resent the fact that this has happened to them and tend to try to find some outside influence on which they can blame the problem. IV. They hope for a magical solution. V. They have come seeking advice. Each of these factors deserves separate consideration by the physician, who must realize that he himself will have certain reactions to the child's condition and to the parents and their emotional problems.

These comments hold true for conditions other than mental retardation, and they hold for helpers other than physicians. These emotional responses, along with the economic and social pressures that are related to the special child, usually necessitate special efforts with the parents as well as the child. These families may require assistance in understanding the disability, the nature of the intervention and their role in it, and particularly in creating expectations which are consistent with the prognosis. Honesty is essential, but it must be conveyed with empathy and understanding. Many parents have had experiences with a "hit-and-run" approach by professionals. They have been given a diagnosis—unfortunately in a manner that borders on the thoughtless—without any assistance. The professional's promise to continue to work with the family and the child in finding the best possible resources can be one of the most reassuring things for parents. The offer to "stand by" and to continue to be available helps prevent the feelings of loneliness and desperation so frequent in parents of handicapped children. Parents may also need assistance in dealing with the variety of professionals who may be involved with their child; i.e., they may need assistance in finding out where to go, what to ask, and what to expect.

The necessity of parental involvement in child-development programs, whether for normal or handicapped children, raises the question: "Who is to work with the parents?" For some time, it was the practice for those who worked with families to have little contact with the parents. In particular circumstances when such isolation seems appropriate, it is in fact neither always necessary nor possible. It would be ideal if all programs could have highly skilled workers available. The absence of such staff, either because they are simply unavailable or because there are not sufficient funds to support them in adequate numbers to meet the needs, does not reduce the necessity for a working relationship with the family.

In this book, specific approaches to such work which can be utilized, depending on available personnel and time, are outlined. There are, however, limitations. Very often a staff is hesitant to invest in parent work because of feelings of inadequacy. Even in the absence of trained workers, funds can at times be found for consultation which can enhance the skills of others. The fact of the matter is that teachers, child-care workers, physical therapists, and many others are forced into these activities by necessity. Though they lack specific training, these people can be tremendously helpful. Their interest, patience, and willingness to listen can be remarkably supportive. An empathic response to the emotional stress of parenthood does not necessarily require extensive training.

In what way can one work with parents? In general, the work may be primarily directed toward a sole parent or couple or toward many parents in group work. Certain parents may have particular needs or desires which may make one or the other (an individual or group) approach more appropriate for them. Some parents feel more comfortable in a group and feel they can get additional help from other group members. On the other hand, a particular parent may be quite disruptive to a group and better seen alone.

Regardless of whether a group or individual approach is used, certain basic patterns in the parent-professional relationship exist. It is of value to be clear about the intent of the parent consultation.

The patterns and methods will vary, depending upon the type of results to be accomplished.

Psychotherapy can be thought of as a process in which there is an intense, often quite dependent relationship between a patient and his therapist. Regression and introspection are encouraged, and often anxiety is created before major changes in behavior begin. In general, there is a nonauthoritarian approach on the part of the therapist.

Counseling can be thought of as a form of supportive therapy in which the relationship between client and counselor is less intense than in psychotherapy, and in which regression is avoided. More effort is likely to be directed to real, current-day problems and feelings than to internal conflict and past experiences.

Guidance is a technique directed specifically at aiding a client in finding ways to set and achieve goals and to avoid conflicts or troublesome situations. This type of consultation depends upon an authoritarian relationship.

Education is a process by which an individual acquires knowledge and develops new abilities to solve problems by careful analysis of a situation. Though education usually involves a teacher and a student, that is not always the case. The goals and the end points of a truly educational effort are mutually set and the pathway not necessarily predetermined.

Training is another approach. Unlike education, training implies the development of specific, predetermined techniques. Any or all of these various patterns can be useful with parents of handicapped children. They may be used in groups or with individuals, but it is important that both worker and parent know what is being done and agree on the goals.

The reader of this book will note considerable overlap between chapters. While the authors have attempted to direct their attention to specific issues regarding the relationship of parents to programs for their children, several themes are common. Trust and respect are basic to all work. Interpersonal relationships depend on several real factors, such as feelings—many of which are beyond awareness—and expectations, some of which are based on hopeful fantasies and upon past experiences. Openness, honesty, and an appreciation for one's feelings and one's concerns are essential. A large measure of the success of a child-development program rests upon the triad of program personnel, parent, and child all working toward the same goal. Our hope in working with parents of handicapped children is that we can assist them through the emotional disorganization that accompanies the recognition of the exceptionality of their child. Our hope with all parents is that we can aid in developing a mature, flexible, concerned adaptation to their children.

Bibliography

Freeberg, N. E., & Payne, D. T. "Parental influence on Cognitive De-velopment in Early Childhood: A Review." *Child Development,* 1967, *38,* 65–87.

The Group for the Advancement of Psychiatry. *Mental Retardation: A Family Crisis—The Therapeutic Role of The Physician* (Report No. 56). Boston: author, 1963.

Kessler, J. W. *Psychopathology of Childhood.* Englewood Cliffs, N.J.: Prentice-Hall, 1966.

Matheny, A. P., Jr., & Vernick, J. "Parents of the Mentally Retarded Child: Emotionally Overwhelmed or Informationally Deprived?" *The Journal of Pediatrics,* 1969, *74,* 953–959.

Pearson, G. H. J. "Some Early Factors in the Formation of Personality." *American Journal of Orthopsychiatry,* 1931, *1,* 284–291.

Solomons, G., & Menolascino, F. J. "Medical Counseling of Parents of the Retarded." *Clinical Pediatrics,* 1968, *7,* 11–16.

Part

The Scope of Parent Programs:

Four Dimensions

Emotional Support for Parents

Hilde S. Schlesinger
Kathryn P. Meadow

When human beings cannot solve a problem, anxiety may develop and a minor problem can become a major crisis. New coping mechanisms can be found by elaborating on the previous ones; trial and error may bring good results. A crisis left too long unresolved can precipitate avoidance of a problem or distortion of a problem, or a breakdown in the individual's usual equilibrium.

Most of us do not face a crisis alone. Fortunately, we have the help of family, friends, neighborhood, community and even nation (Caplan, 1964). An individual in a crisis which affects his usual activities and interpersonal relationships can benefit if another human being can temporarily assume the function of the "helper" and provide emotional support. According to Ross (1964) the personal qualifications of such a helper are more easily listed than acquired. "They include the human qualities of acceptance, understanding and warmth; the professional attributes of objectivity, confidence and knowledge, as well as the technical skill of listening and talking to people under stress [p. 75]."

It is not easy to arrive at a definition of emotional support. In the present context, it might be "that help given to a person in crisis that is designed to restore him to his previous adaptive equi-

HILDE S. SCHLESINGER is Director of Mental Health Services for the Deaf at the Langley Porter Neuropsychiatric Institute in San Francisco. Her areas of special competence are child and community psychiatry and early parent-child interaction.

KATHRYN P. MEADOW is Assistant Project Director and Research Specialist for Mental Health Services for the Deaf at the Langley Porter Neuropsychiatric Institute. She has a strong background in sociology and deaf education.

librium." In addition, we can hope that this emotional support will enable the individual to seek and to find new adaptive mechanisms and to go beyond his old equilibrium in adjusting to the new situation. The ingredients of emotional support include the provision of an opportunity to discuss the problem and the opportunity to meet a helping person who can listen patiently and nonjudgmentally— and who can respond with warmth, honesty, and interest. This helping person can provide knowledge about the crisis effectively and authoritatively, and he can admit ignorance or lack of knowledge confidently and without strain. A helping relationship is most effective when the participants can meet as equal human beings.

Parents in Need of Help

The birth of a normal child into a family is in itself a potential life crisis. The life style of the family members is almost always drastically changed and a readjustment of roles within the family must be achieved. The ability of each family to welcome the arrival of a small, entirely dependent human being depends on the maturity of the parents, their sense of self-esteem as persons and spouses, and their willingness and ability to receive a child of a particular sex and a particular temperament at this specific moment in their lives. The child-to-be is usually seen as an idealized human being who will be able to meet or surpass his parents' achievements and is seen as generally giving pleasure. Nevertheless, from early pregnancy onward the same idealized child may well frustrate some parental needs, evoking resentment on occasion.

The expected idealized child can be seen as a gift to the mother herself, to her husband, or to her parents. If the child is not perfect, latent conflicts are revived even in the most adjusted of parents. During the process of suspecting, recognizing, and identifying a handicap, it would appear that the following emotions are common among parents: shock, bewilderment, sorrow, guilt, and anxiety. Anxiety is a frequent spectre and "tugs" at parental self-esteem and effectiveness prior to the diagnosis, at the time of the diagnosis, and for many months thereafter. The impact of rubella in the early months of pregnancy, the knowledge of Rh incompatibility or of an infectious illness intensifies the usual parental anxieties about the normalcy of their newborn.

Anxiety is an unpleasant emotion characterized by such physiological changes as increased heart rate, breathing, sweating and trembling. This early anxiety is frequently accompanied by parental suspicion that something is amiss with the child and, indeed, parents often reveal themselves to be excellent diagnosticians. Bewilderment and shock occur because of the discrepancy between the expectations and the reality. Sorrow, frequently chronic, may be accompanied by a genuine mourning reaction for the loss of the expected perfect child (Ross, 1964). Guilt feelings, almost always irrational in nature, occur frequently. The parents may ask themselves: "Why did this happen to me?" only to come up with the answer "Because I was bad." Parents often search within themselves for a reason for the defect, a reason which they feel should have been preventable. Such a self-dialogue awakens feelings of resentment and anger directed at the self and at the child. However, negative feelings about a child are unacceptable to most parents and are translated into feelings of guilt.

Parents of any newborn child are faced with a new set of circumstances because the baby has physical and emotional needs. Most new parents have learned something about babyhood and can find ways of coping and satisfying their infant's needs. With a normal infant, growth and development are seen as something predictable, certain, and acceptable, the end result of which is to become an adult much like themselves. Parents of a child with a deficit do not usually have the same opportunity or certainty. These parents want up-to-date and accurate scientific information about the child's condition. They want to know how and when it affects the normal course of child development. Furthermore, these parents want to know what they can do to help their child develop to his capacity and what they may expect this capacity to be. Feelings must be dealt with and ignorance replaced by knowledge.

Many parents cope with the birth of an exceptional child in healthy constructive fashions with a minimum of professional help. They have learned from other crises in their lives how to live with feelings, to tap inner strengths alone, or to accept support from relatives and friends. They have also learned to acquire knowledge through books, articles, and movies. Other parents, however, need professional support both in the area of knowledge acquisition and emotional support. In this, a professional can be of paramount importance to child and parents. She can be the provider of information and emotional support.

The Professional as the Helping Person

Optimally, educational intervention will occur early in the life span of the exceptional child and the professional will meet the parents shortly after the disclosure of the diagnosis. The perspective of the meeting ground may differ for service provider and parent. The professional may be ready and eager to initiate educational or therapeutic techniques, whereas the parent may still be dealing with the impact of the diagnosis or the contact with the experts. The diagnosis of an early childhood defect is a doubly traumatic event both to the parents, who are reluctant to hear it, and to the professionals, who are reluctant to speak of it.

Ineffectual professional stances have resulted from this reluctance. The professional may choose to use the hit-and-run technique, providing the threatening information and leaving the parent laden with feelings and without help. Alternatively, the professional may attempt to deal with parental anxieties by minimizing the problem or by giving false hope; many parents wear rose-colored glasses that were given to them by professionals.

Another ineffective professional ploy is to retire behind a mask of objectivity. However, Beck (1959) and Meadow (1968) have pointed out that parents are more likely to listen and to integrate painful and unpleasant information from interested and compassionate individuals. A professional who leaves the scene or does most of the talking but does not listen is an ineffectual helper.

Listening is the most helpful of all supportive roles. Before providing the necessary information, the professional will need to provide a listening post for the parent; he should be a sensitive human being who is able to listen to the parents calmly, sympathetically, and nonjudgmentally.

The ability to listen to the expression of feelings in nonjudgmental and accepting ways presupposes a knowledge that feelings are always acceptable, though the behavior which springs from them may sometimes be undesirable or detrimental to parent and child. Such careful discrimination between feelings and deeds is helpful to parent and professional. Most parents experience immense relief from really talking about their fears to a concerned professional and need to do this before they can become receptive to acquiring the information that will help them.

A few parents, however, because of a prior emotional disturbance or lack of other support will be overwhelmed by their feelings. Frequently, these parents provoke anxiety in the professional (a signal that the professional himself needs some help). This can often be obtained from a more experienced colleague. Some parents will need more intensive support and may need to be referred for counseling and therapy. The listening professional who is helpful, however, can give adequate emotional support to most parents.

Let us reiterate some of the important qualifications of a helpful person: acceptance, warmth, understanding, genuineness, objectivity, confidence, and knowledge, as well as the ability to listen and talk sensitively with parents under stress. Of paramount importance is honesty in two opposite areas: knowledge and ignorance. Hopefully, the professional will be able to state clearly and comfortably to parents what she does know about their child and, equally comfortably, what she does not know.

Dealing with Feelings

We have previously indicated the myriad of feelings evoked by the birth or diagnosis of an exceptional child. How do parents deal with these feelings? Ideally they will find an opportunity to share the feelings with a supportive person, spouse, parent, friend, or professional, and after a necessary period of mourning, proceed in a rational way to help the child grow to his potential. However, human beings—at least in today's society—are subjected to pressures to behave and feel in an unrealistic fashion. In our early days when something hurts, we are told, "Don't cry—you are not a baby." When events seem tragic, we are told, "Everything will be O.K.— buck up." A vigorous but unsuccessful attempt is often made to banish all uncomfortable feelings. This banishment sometimes occurs by denial—"the tragic event did not happen"—or by repression—banishing from consciousness the feelings or impulses which seem unacceptable. However, the understandable attempt to reduce, translate, or eliminate uncomfortable feelings is not particularly effective. Indeed the attempt often backfires, and the feelings explode with greater intensity.

Sometimes anger springs forth in irrational accusations that the spouse or the doctor is responsible for the child's difficulty. At other times the anger with the child is translated into overly rigid adherence to therapeutic regimens, ostensibly for the child's own good but with a fervor that seems almost punitive. Occasionally, the anger with the child results in parental vacillations between overprotection and overt rejection. Another possible pathway for parental rejection appears to be self-sacrifice and martyrdom for the child's sake. These reactions, performed unconsciously to be sure, are not solutions to the diagnostic crisis. Although it is not the task of the professional to delve into the intricacies of the parent's basic personality or into his unconscious processes (Ross, 1964), the existence of such processes within all of us needs to be kept in mind.

Some basic understanding of the unconscious nature of much of human motivation can be of great benefit to the professional listening and talking to the parent.

Some parents frequently astonish professionals by saying they want advice and then not following it; they say one thing in words and another in behavior. Such a disparity between thinking and behavior has unconscious motivation and is not easily resolved. However, an understanding of the discrepancy usually enables the professional to react with equanimity rather than anger at the contradictory behavior.

In general the professional will be most effective by genuinely accepting the parent's feelings. We stress genuineness, for lip service to acceptance is ineffective. All of us have learned to understand the nonverbal language, and although one may say "I accept what you say," one's true attitude comes through. Acceptance does not necessarily mean approval of everything the parent says or does. It does mean that the professional accepts the parent's feelings that underlie the "unhealthy" feelings or undesirable behavior and that he helps the parent deal with feelings in a constructive fashion.

Again, in summary, a sympathetic, nonjudgmental professional can effectively help most parents in dealing with the feelings evoked by their children. Some parents will need a more intensive form of counseling best offered by mental health consultants. Although it is not easy to clearly differentiate between the two groups in words, the professional can use her own feelings as an indicator. If she is comfortable with her own feelings, she is probably being helpful. However, if her own discomfort is increasing, it is likely that a consultation with a more experienced mental health colleague will be helpful and a decision to refer the parents elsewhere can be reached collaboratively. Some professionals do not have access to mental health consultants and must of necessity make the referral by themselves. Such referrals are always sensitive in nature and are more effective if the professional is able to say, "I am sorry that I cannot be as helpful to you as I wish to be. I would suggest that . . ." She thus places the burden on herself, rather than the parent.

Prescriptions and Proscriptions of Professionals

We have previously outlined the diagnostic crisis, the conflicts between parent and professional and the emotional support provided by the professional in the resolution of this first crisis. The diagnostic crisis is frequently followed by a treatment crisis. Advice given at the time of initiation of treatment can result in a multitude of prescriptions and proscriptions that are, or are perceived to be, overwhelming, conflicting, or incompatible. Furthermore, the advice may revive parental sorrow and fear or may usurp the parents' "right to know" or "right to decide." We shall trace below how the professional may be helpful in each of these eventualities.

Overwhelming Advice.   Parents of children are frequently bombarded by innumerable and bewildering prescriptions. The tasks may be so numerous, so time-consuming, so onerous that the parents become discouraged and feel incapable of ever doing everything required. They may, finally, give up altogether. For example, the parents of a multiply handicapped child—one who may need to wear glasses and hearing aids and orthopedic prostheses—may feel overwhelmed by the multiple prescriptions of experts, one of whom appears to see the eyes alone, another, the ears alone, and another, the limbs alone; the mother sees the whole child. The professional can be supportive by acknowledging frankly that the demands are many, that parents are busy with other responsibilities, and that the practical tasks of parenting a handicapped child at times seem overwhelming. This kind of sympathy, rather than constant stern reminders, can give parents the support and the strength to continue.

Conflicting or Incompatible Advice.   One important area where parents need support that professionals can give is that of resolving differences of opinion between two different professionals representing the same discipline. For example, two audiologists may give differing prescriptions for audiological help. When the teacher feels incapable of advising parents between two different "prescriptions," she can at least acknowledge that she realizes how difficult the situation is for the parents. Then, she can suggest ways for all parties to discuss and resolve the conflict. Perhaps, the teacher could arrange a conference with the conflicting professionals, emphasizing the need for calm discussion of the differences. Often, if parents can vent their feelings about these differences they are better able to approach a consultation with equanimity, eliminating some of the antagonism that makes professionals less able to suggest a compromise. Professionals need some degree of expertise in areas related to their specialty in order to be able to advise parents when this kind of situation arises.

Advice Which Revives Parental Sorrow and Fear.   Professionals
need to be aware that some behavior on the part of parents that
appears to be careless or irresponsible (such as "forgetting" to have
new glasses or hearing aids fitted) is in fact an emotional response
to the sorrow surrounding the diagnosis. For example, a teacher
may encounter a parent who vehemently proclaims an acceptance of
hearing aids yet whose child repeatedly comes to school without
one. A gentle reminder of the discrepancy, followed by sensitive
questions about what happens when the hearing aid is placed on
the child, may elicit feelings of anger at having a visibly defective
child, or anger with professionals who failed to cure the hearing
defect. Such open feelings may enable the parent to behave more
constructively, whereas an exhortation such as, "You know the
child must wear the hearing aid" will only make the parent more
anxious, confused, and defensive. The teacher or counselor may
need to wait until the parent has come to terms with his feelings
before making an issue of the attitudes toward the hearing aid, the
glasses, the crutches, or the wheelchair.

Advice That Usurps Parents' "Right to Know" or "Right to Decide".
Professionals are learning that it is important that they not usurp
parental roles in establishing communication with the child, and
not attempt to substitute their preferred communicative mode, language, or dialect for the one used by the child's family. For example, teachers must guard against usurping parents' "right to know"
of differing approaches to the treatment of the child, and parents'
"right to decide" about the treatment their child receives. The issue
of communicative mode has even greater importance for the deaf
child because the difficulty in learning language is at once the result
and the chief symptom of his handicap. Thus, teachers may face an
important dilemma in offering information and advice about the
choice of oral, manual, or combined forms of communication with
deaf children. Often the solution of the dilemma is reached with the
intent of providing the greatest immediate comfort and support for
parents, but the long-range result can be the opposite of that intended if parents' "right to know" and "right to decide" are not
respected.

Thus teachers of deaf children may avoid telling parents that
there are honest differences of opinion in the area of deaf education, discussing only the method that they themselves prefer. Later,
when parents learn from others about these differences, they may
feel excluded or manipulated, and recriminations from parents are
often heard when the children become older. Secondly, the teacher

may describe alternative methods, but display obvious contempt for those different from her own. The parents then experience conflict, especially where two experts with alternative methods have significant contact with the child. One psychiatric principle espouses the idea that adults may disagree openly about some vital issue without creating conflict or difficulty for the child. However, if the disagreement is accompanied by a lack of respect or even contempt, the child is caught in a conflict he cannot resolve. Thirdly, the teacher may offer complete information about differing methods to parents, may evidence respect for each one, but be reluctant to commit herself to any one method, believing that this increases parental choice. This approach may create ambiguity for parents and the feeling that teachers are unwilling to be completely honest. Sometimes in using this method teachers make vague references to treating individual children by differing methods, and in some instances are reluctant to explain in any general terms the characteristics of the children for whom the individual methods may work best. Parents of very young children can become justifiably impatient with this approach since they cannot always know what their child will be like at a later developmental stage.

In San Francisco, our efforts at parental support in establishing communication include the constant and conscious attempt to diminish conflicts between parents and other professionals that may be related to communicative mode. The most important and basic principle in the area of communication conflicts is that professionals need to find creative ways of encountering others, of sharing controversial information in a relaxed and nonthreatening atmosphere, and of developing genuine respect for opposing points of view.

Achievement of Early Tasks of Social-Emotional Development

Professionals in early-childhood-education programs inevitably become resources for parents in answering questions about childrearing. These questions often seem to require a concrete and definitive reply, but are not answers. There is increasing leeway in "acceptable" child-rearing practices, in regard to the time of introduction of different kinds of foods, the preferred response to a baby's cry, to toilet training, to discipline. Widely varying practices produce well-adjusted and productive children. In most mother-child activities, it seems that it is not the content that makes the differences, but the feeling of comfort that the mother experiences from her unique style, which she then communicates to her child (Schlesinger, 1969).

Thus, one function that the professional can perform is to reinforce parents in continuing the child-rearing practices with which they feel comfortable. Often parents wonder if the things that "feel right" to them in dealing with their nonhandicapped children are also appropriate for their handicapped children. This basic concern is a component of many poignant requests for help with eating, sleeping, and discipline problems. Professionals must be wary of imposing their own cultural or individual biases on their responses to parents' questions. Within this context and with these general points in mind, it is still possible to suggest ways in which professionals can be helpful to parents in terms of emotional support. One of these is the very general point of helping parents in carrying out those child-rearing practices with which they do feel comfortable. Another way to provide support is to give parents an opportunity to discuss their child's behavior and their own responses with a sympathetic, nonjudgmental individual outside the family who has some distance from the immediate day-to-day problems that arise in the home.

In terms of discipline for the young child, one principle that a professional may find helpful is to remind parents that they are usually in a better position to discipline the child if they do not set up conditions that they do not intend to enforce, or that they find impossible to impose. For example, if parents are concerned about a child's eating habits, they might be tempted to tell him that he will not be permitted to leave the table until he has finished the food on his plate. If the child chooses not to finish his dinner, the parent has created a dilemma. The child can outwait the parent if a true battle of wills ensues. If, on the other hand, the parent makes finishing a certain amount of food a condition of receiving dessert, he can give or withhold the sweet.

A recurring theme that parents of handicapped children raise, either implicitly or explicitly, is that of establishing independence. It is a temptation for professionals to assume that parents of handicapped children are "overprotective." Frequently, it is difficult to draw the line between protection that is based on the realistic limitations of the child and protection that is based on parental guilt and anxiety. Again, the opportunity to discuss specific examples with the professional and with other parents can often help parents to arrive at their own definitions of overprotection and realistic caution. The frequent injunction for parents to "treat the handicapped child like any other child" is not truly helpful in cases where the handicap imposes realistic limitations on a child's performance. The failure of professionals to recognize the true limitations imposed by the handicap can result in parents' scaling down their expectations for their normal children, in order to allow themselves to feel that they are treating all the children alike.

Finally, a frequent concern of parents with whom we work is that of handling temper tantrums effectively. In this area, there seems to be a wide range of behaviors that individual parents feel comfortable about accepting. One mother described how she successfully discouraged tantrums by putting a drop of Tabasco sauce on her finger and touching it to the child's tongue. Another mother told of putting a child under a shower fully clothed to discourage a temper tantrum; a week later the child placed herself under the shower apparently in an effort to stop herself from a fit of temper. Both of these tactics made some parents uncomfortable, while others viewed them as interesting possibilities for future reference. It is important for professionals to find ways of saying to parents, "This may not be my way, but if you feel comfortable about it, if the child does not suffer, I will accept your way of behaving and hope you can accept mine."

Expectations for Present and Future

An understandable parental desire for the child to be like them or to surpass them in achievements is often accompanied by a massive attempt to make the child normal. Sometimes these wishes result in an effort to eliminate the handicap itself and the differences that it causes. Certainly the effect of a handicap can be diminished by early intervention and education, but the deaf child typically does not become like a hearing child. The blind child does not become like a sighted child; the retarded child does not become like a normal child. Exhortations to become normal are frequently seen by the child as "nonacceptance," not only of his handicap, but of his very being.

Two main tasks fall to the professional working with the young child with a deficit. One is to provide a realistic, nonrosy but nonsomber, picture of the achievement and adjustment of adults with a similar handicap. This can be established by providing literature and also more importantly, through contact with adults of similar backgrounds. For example, successful deaf adults can provide a spurt of hope and self-esteem to parents and deaf children. It may be true that many hearing parents will have a traumatic reaction to adult deaf speech, but we feel that this will be transient and less detrimental than a failure to acknowledge reality. Many parents of older youngsters known to us have expressed deep regret for the years when they held tenaciously to the belief that their deaf child would grow into a seemingly hearing youngster. They now feel that this distorted expectation interfered with effective early parenting.

The second task of the professional is to help the parents diminish their attempts to mold the child into normalcy. For instance, in their poignant search for speech, many parents extend the training of the child far beyond his physical or emotional capabilities. The expectations for speech also frequently result in maneuvers on the part of the parents that evoke massive negativism toward speech or even eye contact with the parent. In general, a professional can sensitively explore what normalcy means to the parent, place normalcy into a realistic realm, and provide steps that will be effective and not counterproductive. She can help the parent to understand that while a handicap is not the only thing that matters, it continues to be important. Other characteristics are more important: a child is always "a child first," although a handicap produces additional needs in both the child and the parent.

Bibliography

Beck, H. L. "Counseling Parents of Retarded Children." *Children,* 1959, *6,* 225–230

Boles, G. "Personality Factors in Mothers of Cerebral Palsied Children." *Genetic Psychology Monographs,* 1959, *59.*

Caplan, G. *Principles of Preventive Psychiatry.* New York: Basic Books, 1964.

Erikson, E. H. *Identity and the Life Cycle.* New York: International Universities Press, 1959.

Erikson, E. H. *Childhood and Society.* New York: Norton, 1963.

Erikson, E. H. *Identity, Youth and Crisis.* New York: Norton, 1968.

Farber, B. Effects of a Severely Mentally Retarded Child on Family Integration." *Monographs of the Society for Research in Child Development,* 1959, *24* (No. 2).

Fellendorf, G., & Harrow, I. "Parent Counseling 1961–1968." *Volta Review,* 1970, *72,* 51–57.

Meadow, K. P. "Parental Response to The Medical Ambiguities of Congenital Deafness." *Journal of Health and Social Behavior,* 1968, *9,* 299–309.

Pettigrew, T. F. *A Profile of the Negro American.* Princeton: Van Nostrand, 1964.

Ross, A. O. *The Exceptional Child in the Family.* New York: Grune and Stratton, 1964.

Schlesinger, H. S. "A Child First." *Volta Review,* 1969, *71,* 545–551.

Schlesinger, H. S., & Meadow, K. P. *Sound and Sign: Childhood Deafness and Mental Health.* Berkeley: University of California Press, 1972.

Wright, B. A. *Physical Disability—A Psychological Approach.* New York: Harper and Row, 1960.

Exchanging Information

Janis Jelinek
Andrea Yates Kasper

Information exchange may best be defined as a process by which parents become cognitively aware through interaction with others (e.g., teachers) of the many aspects of their child's world. It usually takes place through formal professional-parent contact. To be most effective, the information exchanged needs to be imparted in a planned systematic manner. The exchange should begin with the program staff informing the parents about the rationale, objectives, and activities of the program in which their child is enrolled.

The necessity of clear communication dictates that the program be well conceived before it is put into operation. This involves the consideration of four elements: parent input, program constraints, design, and evaluation. The central element, program design, must include ways of communicating information to the parents on the following topics: normal development, handicapping conditions, behavior management, and intervention procedures, materials, and equipment. This information is vital to the parent in both the home and center situation.

JANIS JELINEK is Director of the University of Wyoming's (Laramie) Communicative Disorders and Parent Training Program, an Assistant Professor of Speech Pathology, and the Director of the University's (HCEEP) Outreach Project. Her areas of interest include: language problems in preschool children, paraprofessional training, and parent programming.

ANDREA YATES KASPER is a speech pathologist at the Veterans Administration Hospital in Sheridan, Wyoming. Her primary professional interest is language problems in the preschool and school-age child.

Parent Input

During the initial planning stages of a parent program, it is neces-sary to determine what kind of information the parents feel is im-portant. Before the University of Wyoming parent program was initiated, we sent a needs-assessment questionnaire to all potential participants asking them to rate as very important, important, or not very important a list of program suggestions. Space was also provided on the questionnaire for additional topical suggestions. The parents were assured that the information they provided would serve as group data only and their answers would remain confiden-tial (see Figure 4).

The ratings served as a basis for structuring our parent pro-gram. This particular checklist (Figure 4) was structured for the par-ents of speech-, hearing-, and language-impaired children but could easily be adapted to parents of children with any or no hand-icap.

If a program is to be successful, assessment of parent needs must be a continuing process. There are a number of possible ways to obtain information for this reassessment. One is from verbal comments made by the parents. The second is by administering questionnaires which are completed at regular intervals during the program. The third is to form a parent advisory council to meet regularly to help with programming suggestions. The parent advi-sory council which has voting power on policy decisions should be made up of three or four parents from differing socio-demographic levels. Our parent-advisory council, for example, helped us formu-late one of our questionnaires. Those who are initiating parent infor-mation programs should plan to use all three of these methods—verbal comments from parents, questionnaires, and a parent advi-sory council—for conducting their needs assessment. With this type of information, it is possible for the staff to continually restructure a more effective parent information program.

Program Constraints

In designing a parent information program, professionals must con-sider physical, economic, and psychological constraints. For exam-ple, it may be difficult for parents to participate on a regular basis because there may be siblings in the home that the parents cannot leave in order to attend the program. Consideration should be given to providing day care or baby-sitting services for these

Figure 4

Needs Assessment

Below are listed ten suggested areas of instruction for parent training in our expanded summer clinic program. Please rate each area on its importance to you as parents. Place a check in the appropriate box.

	Very Important	Important	Not Very Important
1. Assisting in group activities with the children such as creative play, arts and crafts, swimming and snack programs.	___	___	___
2. Observing your child's therapy sessions.	___	___	___
3. Participating in group parent counseling sessions.	___	___	___
4. Learning to assist in your child's therapy.	___	___	___
5. Participating in individual parent counseling sessions.	___	___	___
6. Receiving information about all aspects of normal child development.	___	___	___
7. Receiving information about speech, hearing and language disorders.	___	___	___
8. Receiving information about normal speech and language development.	___	___	___
9. Learning to cope with your child's specific problems.	___	___	___
10. Receiving an explanation of evaluation procedures used for identifying speech, hearing or language disorders.	___	___	___

Other suggestions for programming will be appreciated. Please be specific.

Name _____

Child's Name _____ Child's Birthdate_____

Mailing Address _____

Telephone_____

Please fill out the information above and return in a self-addressed stamped envelope.

I am interested in applying for this program for my child and myself.

siblings. Perhaps the lack of transportation to and from the center may prevent some parents from participating. The solution to this problem may require not only making arrangements for transportation but also providing monies for transportation. Also, it is important to remember that the inclusion of as many family members as possible in the program increases the use and effectiveness of the information in the home setting. Whenever possible, not only mothers, but fathers, grandparents, and older siblings should be invited to participate.

Problems in program delivery represent another constraint. To deal with these, a decision-making or planning process must be incorporated as an ongoing activity. It is important to involve as many people as possible in this process—parents, staff, and director. Decision-making or planning must be carried out in regard to such delivery issues as (1) the frequency of the information-giving sessions, (2) the coordination of staff members presenting information—who will do what and when, (3) the sequence and continuity of information to coordinate with other facets of parent-child programming, (4) the arrangement for audiovisual and supplementary materials to be available when needed, and (5) the consideration of how the information is going to be used by the parents and other family members in the home setting.

Program Design

From our experience in working with parents, we feel that the following areas should be included in information exchange programming: (1) information concerning the rationale, objectives, and activities of both the parent and child programs; (2) information on normal development; (3) information about handicapping conditions in children; (4) information about behavior modification; (5) exposure to and/or experience with intervention procedures, materials, and equipment which can be used in the clinical situation or home setting; and (6) follow-up into the home setting.

In designing our parent information program for items one through six, we found it necessary to collect programming ideas from many sources; in many cases, we developed our own ideas. The following is an overview of methods and materials incorporated into our parent-information program.

Information About the Program. Parents should be informed initially and continually about the rationale, objectives, and activities of the program in which their child is enrolled. We have used an intensive eight-week training session during the summer to initiate necessary information exchanges.

Normal Development.   One of the most helpful programs that we have found for presenting the concept of normal development is the workshop series, *Teach Your Child to Talk* (Pushaw, Collins, Czuchna, Gill, O'Betts, and Stahl, 1969). This program includes a general overview, materials for three workshops, and an evaluation form. The first workshop deals with normal development in infants from birth to twelve months; the second workshop deals with normal development from twelve months to three years; the third deals with normal development from three to five years. Each of these workshops is designed to cover about two hours' time. However, one can easily break each of the workshops into several segments to cover two or three different parent meetings. The materials included in the kit are: slides, tape recordings, a 16mm color film, a workshop manual, a set of pamphlets entitled *Teach Me to Talk* (Czuchna, 1969), and a parent handbook. The pamphlets and handbook may be purchased in quantity. Depending upon the frequency of this kind of presentation in your program, these materials may be all that is needed for presenting information on normal development.

Since our program is scheduled for eight intensive weeks during the summer, we have found it is necessary to include additional materials such as *Parents' Magazine's Child Development* and *Family Living Filmstrips* (1974), *Human Development-Child Development Filmstrip Packages* (Concept Media, 1974/75), *Home-Based Preschool Education* (Olympus Publishing, 1974), *Beginning Concepts-Filmstrip Program in Basic Concepts and Perceptions* (Scholastic Early Childhood Center, 1974), and *Brushing Up on Parenthood Series* (Cahoon, Price, and Scoresby, 1974). Additionally, there are many low-cost films, pamphlets, and other materials (Metropolitan Life, 1970; Children's Bureau, 1968; Johnson, 1953; Boone, 1965; Jung, 1968) which are available commercially for use in parent-information programs. Dittoed handouts on various aspects of normal development (such as speech, language, social, and emotional) may also be compiled for dissemination to parents.

Another method for providing information about child development and functioning is to involve parents as aides in various activities such as swimming, playground, and arts and crafts. Here parents can gain information by observing and interacting with the children in relatively normal types of activities. Through this aspect of the program parents are given a chance to apply their classroom knowledge with the children they work with and observe.

Handicapping Conditions.   The types of children enrolled in our program are those with speech, hearing, and language handicaps. Therefore, the information we give to our parents about handicapping conditions relates primarily to these disorders. A selection of materials for information on handicapping conditions includes: (1) films (Harper and Row, 1970; Clarke School, 1970; MISSCA, 1968; University of Iowa, 1956); (2) pamphlets (NIH, 1970; Northcott, 1970; Pennington, Corbin, and James, 1966; Sayre, 1966); and (3) other references (Irwin, 1968; Battin and Haug, 1968; Van Riper, 1961; Johnson, ed., 1958; Screiber, 1956). Dittoed materials on handicapping conditions may be used for handouts for parents. Not only do we use these and other materials in our group sessions, but we also have them available to loan to parents for use at home.

Another effective method for informing parents about handicapping conditions is through the use of videotape. With the parents' permission, we videotaped various children in actual therapy sessions and used this tape as a springboard for discussion concerning the etiology and ramifications of various speech, hearing, and language disorders.

Behavior Modification.   Information about behavior modification serves a two-fold purpose in our program: (1) it provides the parents with methods for managing such behaviors as whining, temper tantrums, and fear in the home setting; and (2) it serves as a background for the parents in observing, baselining, reinforcing, and graphing behavior.

The basic tool we use in this phase of our program is *Living With Children: New Methods for Parents and Teachers* (Patterson and Gullion, 1971). This book is written in the form of programmed instruction and teaches parents to understand and manage behavior which is distressing to them. A second programmed text that we found to be valuable is *Parents Are Teachers: A Child-Management Program* (Becker, 1971).

A number of other pamphlets, films, and books are also made available to the parents in this program. The selection of these materials must be necessarily dependent upon the philosophy of the individual program.

Intervention Procedures, Materials, and Equipment. This content area is included in our program to give our parents a basis for working with their children not only in the clinical situation but in the home. We give information about and practice in using such materials as the *Peabody Language Development Kit* (Dunn and Smith, 1965, 1966, 1968); the *Distar Language Program* (Englemann, Osborn, and Englemann, 1969); and *Learning to Develop Language Skills* (Sprugel, Nice, and Karnes, 1970). We also provide basic information about various instruments that are used to evaluate the children to help the parents understand the results of our evaluations.

We also give parents opportunities to develop and create materials for use in the home situation. In our monthly newsletter, parents receive lists of materials to collect and bring to the summer session. The clinicians assist the parents in individualizing these materials according to their child's needs. A side-effect of creating these materials is that the parents develop skills in (1) making dittoed materials and transparencies, and (2) learning to use various pieces of equipment such as the veri-fax machine, laminating machine, and opaque projector. The parents are also instructed and have practice in using audio and videotape equipment and slide and movie projectors.

Follow-up. Follow-up, or visits in the home setting, may be an integral part of an ongoing parent program, or it may be a type of activity which follows intensive programming for parents. In Wyoming, our follow-up took place after our eight week summer programming experience.

Home visits cover not only parent information but all aspects of parent-child programming. They provide an ideal time to observe the parent-child interaction in the home setting; for example, what kinds of discipline is the parent using with the child, what kinds of stimulation is the parent giving the child. These visits are helpful and necessary to answer questions or to help solve problems that the parent may be having. Dependent upon program philosophy, this is also the time to work cooperatively with the parents in developing objectives for home training. The person who is making the home visits should demonstrate to the parents the skills the child is expected to develop before the next visit and review any materials which will be used in the program. Continued dissemination of materials and information is another aspect of home visits. This is particularly important when the parents do not live within commuting distance of the center.

Program Evaluation

In this age of accountability, it is important to determine how effective a program is. In evaluating any facet of parent programming, it is important to convey to the parents that they are not necessarily being evaluated but that the effects of the program are being assessed.

In evaluating the effectiveness of our program, we use several instruments. Our parents are given the Parent Attitude Research Inventory (Schaefer and Bell, 1958) upon entering the program. They also fill out a feedback questionnaire which is rated on the Likert scale (see Figure 5). Those who are initiating programs will want to develop their own scales which are pertinent to the objectives and activities of their own program. It is not really important whether the scale is based on 1–5 or if it is just a questionnaire which requires "yes," "no," or "no opinion" answers. The importance of a scale lies in the fact that staff and/or parents have had a hand in its evolution.

During the actual programming, the parents are asked to complete a weekly pre- and post-study guide (Figure 6). To assess their understanding of the program, we utilize a checklist which is filled out when the parents observe our clinicians working with their child. Finally, we assess the overall program by using Figures 7 and 8.

In the home setting, we assess the effectiveness of both our programming and parents through the use of learning packets (Caster, Dublinski, and Grimes, 1972). These packets are structured so that the parents will know exactly what their responsibilities are, how to carry out the program, and when the program should be completed. This is accomplished through an intervention process which involves writing supportive instructional objectives and specific educational recommendations. With the supportive instructional objectives, there is a clear method for monitoring progress; thus, feedback can be provided on the effectiveness of the recommendations which increases the probability that the objective will be carried out by the parent.

In order to keep any program "on target," evaluation must be an integral aspect. It is important to remember that if parents do not understand our information it is the fault of our programming and not the fault of the parents.

Figure 5

Feedback Questionnaire

Directions: Please rate yourself as fairly and accurately as possible on the following questions. A scale from 1 to 5 is provided with (1) being the lowest or
poor, and (5) being the highest or excellent. Circle the rating you believe would
be closest to your knowledge or ability.

1. Knowledge of normal speech and language development:

        1   2   3   4   5

2. Knowledge of speech and language disorders:

        1   2   3   4   5

3. Understanding of behavior-modification techniques:

        1   2   3   4   5

4. Ability to assist my child in overcoming his/her speech problem:

        1   2   3   4   5

5. Opinion of the follow-up program:

        1   2   3   4   5

The administration desires to judge the effectiveness of the program for improving future programs, and your help will be greatly appreciated.

Figure 6

Pre and Post Study Guide for Normal Development

1. The infant's vocalizations during the first two to three weeks of life are termed:

    a. gurgling
    b. cooing
    c. reflexive
    d. differential
    e. linguistic

2. True speech:

    a. is developed
    b. begins somewhere between the 12th and 18th month
    c. does not begin until the child understands speech
    d. a and c
    e. a, b, and c

3. At about six or seven weeks of age, the infant begins to show by his reactions that he is aware of the sounds he is making. This is termed:

    a. awareness
    b. babbling
    c. responsiveness
    d. reactionary
    e. maturation

4. At about nine or ten months of age, the child may be heard imitating sounds which others have made, and which are prevalent in his environment. This is termed:

    a. environmental reaction
    b. imitation
    c. echolalia
    d. bradylalia
    e. acalculia

5. _____ is defined as repetition of heard sounds or sound combinations.

    a. perservation
    b. proprioception
    c. idioglossia
    d. lalling
    e. kinesthesia

6. When a child has developed "inner language," we say he has developed:

    a. thinking
    b. inflection
    c. occlusion
    d. internalization

7. When a child has developed "receptive language," we say he:

    a. receives
    b. lateralizes
    c. operates
    d. understands
    e. commentates

8. When a child develops "expressive language," we say that:

    a. he says one or two words
    b. he must have first developed inner and receptive language.
    c. he has also developed all of his motor skills
    d. a and b
    e. a, b, and c

Figure 6 (Continued)

9. Before each of the following, put an *A* if the normal development occurs between 12 to 18 months; a *B* if the normal development occurs between 18 to 24 months; a *C* if the normal development occurs between 2—3 years; a *D* if the normal development occurs between 3 to 4 years; or an *E* if the normal development occurs between 4 to 5 years.

_____ has completed 90 percent of the job of learning how to talk.

_____ will (1) distort a sound or substitute one sound for another or (2) completely leave a sound out of a word.

_____ is eager to learn names for everything.

_____ frequently uses two—word sentences.

_____ is able to understand most of what you say in its complicated adult form.

_____ uses jargon.

_____ may exhibit normal nonfluency.

_____ may play with sounds by rhyming words.

_____ sentences average 4—5 words.

_____ can tell you what he wants by pointing and saying a few words.

10. Check the activity below which would *least* likely be included in a parent involvement/ training program dealing with handicapped children.

_____ information about normal development

_____ opportunities to make materials for home training

_____ "awareness" groups

_____ information about handicapping conditions

_____ opportunities to observe and assist in their child's training program

_____ training in counting behaviors and behavior modification

_____ information about nutrition and opportunities to learn to prepare balanced meals

_____ working as aides in supplementary programs for children

11. Check the materials or equipment below (3) which would be *least* useful in training parents of handicapped children.

_____ *Living With Children* by Patterson and Gullion

_____ "Dr. Spock"

_____ *Getting Ready to Read* published by Houghton Mifflin

_____ *Parent Attitude Research Inventory* by Sheafer and Bell

_____ Video—tape equipment

_____ Sewing machine, cotton material, socks, arts and crafts materials

_____ Golf counters

_____ *Better Homes and Gardens Cookbook*

Figure 7

Communicative Disorders & Parent Training Program

Questionnaire

	Yes	No

1. Do you feel that you benefited from the Communicative Disorders and Parent Training Program?   _____   _____

   Have you been able to use the knowledge you gained this summer?   _____   _____

2. Do you feel that your child benefited from the Communicative Disorders and Parent Training Program?   _____   _____

   Has your child continued to show progress since returning home? If not, please explain.   _____   _____

3. Children's Program:

   Do you feel that your child had enough individual therapy sessions?   _____   _____

   Do you feel that your child benefited from the group language sessions? If your answer is no, please explain.   _____   _____

Please list other changes you would like to see made in the children's program.

4. Parent Program:

   Class Organization:

   Would you like to see more formal lectures by staff members?   _____   _____

   Would you like to have more parents' participation in planning or programs?   _____   _____

   Would you like to have smaller groups?   _____   _____

   Therapy Materials:

   Do you think a Parent Committee should help plan and oversee making of materials?   _____   _____

   Do you think materials should be more geared to child's age and problem?   _____   _____

Please comment on other changes you would like to see regarding construction of materials.

Observing and assisting in therapy:

   How many days of instruction do you feel you need before beginning observation?

   _____ 2 days; _____5 days; _____10 days; _____other? (state)

   Do you feel it is important to begin by observing children other than your own?   _____   _____

Figure 7 (Continued)

How many days do you feel that you need to observe before beginning
to assist in therapy?

_____ 5 days; _____ 7 days; _____ 10 days; _____ other (state) _____

Please comment on other changes you would like to see regarding observing
and assisting in therapy.

	Yes	No
Volunteers for swimming, arts and crafts, and playground:		
Should a committee of parents be involved in planning the above activities?	_____	_____
Please comment on other changes you would like to see in these programs.	_____	_____
Teacher–parent relationship:		
Would you like to have a definite time schedule each week to meet with your child's therapist?	_____	_____
Do you need more help from the teachers in planning therapy activities?	_____	_____

Please make other comments as to how the teachers can be more helpful in the parent training program.

5. Would you like to see a definite time scheduled each week for each
   individual mother to meet with the psychologist?   _____ _____

6. Would you like to see the discussion groups with Mrs. Boyer (social
   worker) continued?   _____ _____

7. We are particularly anxious to learn how we can make dorm life a more
   pleasant experience. Please make suggestions for improving this aspect
   of the program.

8. Where did you hear about the Communicative Disorders and Parent
   Training Program? What suggestions would you make for informing
   other parents about this program?

9. Follow–up Program:

   Do you feel that members of the follow–up staff are visiting you often
   enough to be helpful?   _____ _____

   Have staff suggestions been helpful to you?   _____ _____

   Have arrangements for other services for your child (regular speech
   therapy, physical therapy, etc.) been satisfactory? If no, please
   explain.   _____ _____

Please make other comments for improving the follow–up program (on back).

Please make other comments for improving the follow–up program (on back).

Figure 8
Program Evaluation

1. As a result of participating in this program, I feel that my child:

   Has shown improvement in speech and language skills _____

   Has shown little or no improvement in speech and language skills _____

   Please explain:

2. As a result of participating in this program, I feel that I (as a parent):

   Have gained in my understanding of my child's disability and my ability to help him _____

   Have gained little or no new understanding of my child's disability and feel no better able to help him with it than I was before I came to the workshop _____

   Please explain:

3. What parts of the program did you find to be most helpful and why?

4. What parts of the program did you find to be least helpful and why?

5. What changes would you recommend to be made in the program for next year?

Please check one of the following:

_____ I participated in almost all of the program.

_____ I missed more than five days of the program (or did not participate in full day sessions.)

_____ I participated in less than half of the program.

Bibliography

Battin, R., & Haug, C. O. *Speech and Language Delay: A Home Training Program.* Springfield, Ill: Charles C. Thomas, 1968.

Becker, W. *Parents Are Teachers: A Child-Management Program.* Chicago: Research Press, 1971.

Boone, D. R. *Infant Speech and Language Development.* Washington: Volta Bureau, 1965.

Bryant, J. *Helping Your Child Speak Correctly.* Public Affairs, 1970, No. 445.

Cahoon, O., Price, A., & Scoresby, A. *Brushing Up on Parenthood Series* (film). Provo, Utah: Brigham Young University, Institute of Family Home Education, 1974.

Caster, J., Dublinski, S., and Grimes, J. *Increasing Intervention Effectiveness Through Improved Communication.* Des Moines: State Department of Education, Special Education, 1972.

Cavendish, M. *Story of Life.* London: Author, 1969–70.

Clark School. *Everything But Hear* (film). Northampton: author, 1970.

Concept Media. *Human Development-Child Development Filmstrip Packages.* Costa Mesa, California: Author, 1974–1975.

Czuchna, G. *Teach Me to Talk.* New York: CEBCO Standard Publishing Co., 1969.

Dorley, F., & Van Riper, C. *Introduction to Speech Problems* (film). Detroit: Wayne State University, 1965.

Dunes, P., & Pinson, E. N. *The Speech Chain* (film). Murray Hill, New Jersey: Bell Telephone Laboratories, 1964.

Dunn, L., & Smith, J. O. *Peabody Language Development Kit No. 1.* Circle Pines, Minnesota: American Guidance Service, 1965.

Dunn, L., & Smith J. O. *Peabody Language Development Kit No. 2.* Circle Pines, Minnesota: American Guidance Service, 1966.

Dunn, L., & Smith, J. O. *Peabody Language Development Kit No. 3.* Circle Pines, Minnesota: American Guidance Service, 1968.

Englemann, S., Osborn, J., & Englemann, T. *Distar Language I.* Chicago: Science Research Associates, 1969.

Harper and Row. *Language Disorders* (film). New York: Author, 1970.

Harper and Row. *Articulation Disorders* (film). New York: Author, 1970.

Irwin, R. B. *A Speech Pathologist Talks to Parents and Teachers.* Pittsburgh: Stanevix House, 1968.

Johnson, W. *Is My Child Normal: An Open Letter to a Normal Mother and Father.* Danville, Illinois: Interstate, 1968.

Johnson, W. *Speech Problems in Children.* New York: Harper and Row, 1953.

Jung, C. *Inner World of Childhood.* New York: Signet Books, 1968.

Long, C. L. *Will Your Child Learn to Talk Correctly?* Danville, Illinois: Interstate, 1968.

Metropolitan Life Insurance Company. *If These Were Your Children* (film). New York: Author, 1970.

Minnesota Society for Crippled Children and Adults. *Seven for Suzie* (film). Minneapolis: Author, 1968.

National Institute of Health. *Learning to Talk.* Bethesda, Maryland: Hinds, 1970.

Northcott, W. Reading list for parents. *Volta Review,* 1971, *73,* 186–189.

Olympus Publishing Company. *Home-Based Preschool Education* (film). Salt Lake City: Author, 1974.

Parent's Magazine Films, Inc. *Parent's Magazine Child Development and Family Living Filmstrips.* New York: Author, 1974.

Patterson, G. & Gullion, M. E. *Living With Children: New Methods for Parents.* Champaign, Illinois: Research Press, 1971.

Pennington, R., & James, E. *For the Parents of a Child Whose Speech Is Delayed.* Danville, Illinois: Interstate, 1966.

Pushaw, D., Collins, N., Czuchna, G., Gill, G., O'Betts, G., & Stahl, M. *Teach Your Child to Talk.* Cincinnatti: CEBCO Standard Publishing Co., 1969.

Sayre, J. M. *Helping the Child to Listen and Talk.* Danville, Illinois: Interstate, 1966.

Schaefer, E. S., & Bell, R. Q. "Development of a Parental Attitude Instrument." *Child Development*, 1958, *29*, 339–362.

Scholastic Early Childhood Center. *Beginning Concepts: Filmstrip Program in Basic Concepts and Perceptions.* Englewood, New Jersey: Author, 1974.

Screiber, F. R. *Your Child's Speech: A Practical Guide for Parents for the First Five Years.* New York: G. P. Putnam, 1956.

Sprugel, C., Nance, I. D., & Karnes, M. B. *Learning to Develop Language Skills.* Springfield, Massachusetts: Milton Bradley, 1970.

United States Department of Health, Education, and Welfare. *Your Child from 1–6.* Washington: Children's Bureau Publications, 1968.

University of Iowa. *Children with Cleft Palates.* Iowa City: Author, 1970.

Van Riper, C. *Your Child's Speech Problems.* New York: Author, 1961.

Developing Parent Participation

Winifred H. Northcott
Shirley A. Fowler

Parents and professionals are developing genuine partnerships today in an increasing number of early childhood education programs. These valuable and productive relationships can be facilitated through the design and implementation of programs to meet the needs of parents as well as the needs of the children. When parents are offered the opportunity in a professional setting to gain insight into the ways that young children learn and into the nature of the parent role in "care giving," three processes are involved. (These processes were labeled by Dr. Murray Reed, Supervising Psychologist at the Wilder Child Guidance Clinic in St. Paul, Minnesota.) First, there is *an exchange of information between the partners* (teacher and parents) before actual communication begins. This exchange covers items such as each child's developmental history, the family's social history and certain test results. Second, the *parents are encouraged to grow in their role.* They are offered the opportunity to practice new ways of behaving in daily child management. Here, spontaneity, honesty, and openness are essential. One way to en-

WINIFRED H. NORTHCOTT is the "Early Childhood Education for the Handicapped" consultant at the Minnesota Department of Education and the Director of the UNISTAPS Project (HCEEP) in Minneapolis-St. Paul. Her major area of interest is education for the hearing-impaired child, and her specialties within the area are parent training and mainstreaming.

SHIRLEY A. FOWLER is a doctoral student at the University of Minnesota who is enrolled in the Psycho-educational studies program. Her major interests are the young child with special needs and his family. She has had extensive experience as a teacher, lecturer, and consultant in the area of developing programs for the families of young handicapped children.

65

courage behavioral changes in parents is to offer them the role of co-experimenter, of observing or teaching a child other than their own. Placement in the "right" group of parents is also useful. The third process is *building a trusting, productive relationship between the parents and teachers* which will enable parents to regain their own sense of playfulness and to feel satisfied with the quality of daily interactions between themselves and their child in a home-care setting.

A Rationale for Parent Participation

During the vulnerable preschool years, a young child's behavior reflects the emotional climate in his home. The quality of parental responses to his predictable requirements encourages or limits the child's later development of social skills, emotional stability, and intellectual productivity (Erikson, 1963).

The basic premises underlying parent participation are that (1) parents benefit from active involvement in a preschool program because they can expand their parenting skills; (2) increased involvement is useful to parents in developing a successful identity which includes a feeling of personal worth; this identity is a prerequisite for a stimulating home environment in which maximum listening, sharing and learning take place; and (3) parents learn as well from each other as they do from a professional staff.

Potential Barriers to Parent Participation

Active parent participation in the educational program of a young child is the responsibility of the professional. Parent participation is but one component of a comprehensive program of guidance, counseling, and education for parents—which requires an interdisciplinary team effort for implementation. Only as a parent is helped to understand his feelings and attitudes about a new child, can a natural, affectionate parent-child relationship develop. Parent participation is one way of increasing the parents' confidence about, and competence in, daily home training and effective child management.

The solo parent, the parent in a multigeneration family under one roof, and the working parent require modifications in the timing and content of scheduled involvement in their children's programs to fit their life styles, cultural traditions, and working patterns. Other factors also affect parental response to available services. For example, the parents' orientation is important. Any professional who carefully observes parents can recognize the "selective listener" or the parents who keep on "shopping" for new cures and more sympathetic ears to listen to unmet needs. There are also well-educated mothers and fathers who manipulate information from "the literature" to their own advantage, without attending to its practical application within the home. There is the very young parent who may reject the authority of "the establishment" in general.

There is the mother and father who have transferred from another program and require time to adjust to the values, the goals, and the objectives of the new program as well as to the activities in which they are expected to participate. There are parents who have known only one or two handicapped individuals, parents who misunderstand the orientation of the program. There are also interpersonal problems, such as marital difficulties, which affect the child who needs the security of parental assistance and emotional support. But individuals do change in attitudes and actions if they feel free to make up their own minds and reach their own conclusions about new ways of handling themselves and their children.

Once enrolled, parental growth through active participation is fostered in *all* mothers and fathers or parent surrogates regardless of their personal circumstances. A parent with little formal education, the bilingual parent, or any other parent will respond to the challenge of growth if the belief that people *can* change is instilled. For this reason, suitable adaptations are required to insure that every parent is an active participant during group and individual meetings.

Parental Roles

Parents might assume a variety of roles during active participation in the preschool child's educational program. They include: the parent as an individual, the parent as a learner, the parent as an informal teacher, and the parent as a partner of the schools.

The Parent as an Individual.   It must be recognized that parents are individuals with personal motivations, needs, aspirations, and ideals. Parents need to feel accepted and need someone who will listen with an empathetic ear without judging or without necessarily giving advice. The parent of a handicapped child should be encouraged to move toward the solution of personal conflict by expressing his attitudes and feelings about having a handicapped child.

The Parent as a Learner.   By sharing information and receiving support in an individual or group setting, parents can develop realistic expectations for themselves which are based upon knowledge of the behavioral characteristics of young children. Parenting skills can be greatly enhanced through information on child development, toilet training techniques, and controlling behavior. It may also be helpful for parents to learn teaching techniques such as procedures for developing language in connection with child-centered activities in the home. There are many excellent written materials for parents which can be collected for a parent resource library. Films and other audiovisual materials are useful in providing parents with information.

Observation of their child in classroom situations can give parents insight into the child's interactions with other adults, his level of skill development, the nature of effective teaching techniques, and how new or familiar materials can be used. Observations should be guided and explained by a staff member for this to be a useful experience for parents.

The Parent as a Teacher.   This role is assumed when there is an interaction of parent, teacher, and child in an experiential activity, and where the parent gradually assumes the lead role under direction. Such activity encourages parents to be more confident about their skills and more competent in making use of daily care times for natural listening experiences and spontaneous self-expression.

Initial educational intervention should include a regular schedule of visits with parents and children, which are offered either in the family home, the school, or a demonstration home setting. If the mothers work, relatives or babysitters may participate. Siblings who are present can be included periodically in the activities, or supervised in play by a volunteer or teacher aide. This period enables a teacher to observe language and social interaction between parent and child during a shared activity. Periodic videotaping enables parents to make certain observations about their teaching style and the child's responses. The parents and teachers should take the opportunity to describe observed behavioral changes. The topics discussed will range widely, and may be supplemented by quotes from the mother's notebook. Most parents enjoy sharing anecdotes. "When I pretended I was going to sit on

Leslie's chair this morning," reported one mother, "she pointed to my fanny and said, 'Too bih (big)' and pointed to the chair, saying 'too 'mall!' '" "How logical she is," replied the teacher, "and how great you think it's funny! You care more about what Leslie's trying to tell you than how well she says it, at this point. That's just right!"

A parent's questions should be noted in a teacher's weekly progress report *after* the visit is concluded, along with samples of the child's receptive and expressive language and the highlights of adult and child behavior. This informal developmental log is a handy reference during the writing of behavioral objectives for each parent and child. Later on, the interval of time between these visits may be increased while still maintaining optimal usefulness. You should plan also for parent involvement in the individual teaching program which must supplement a child's group educational experiences around the age of three years.

The Parent as Partner of the Schools.   The most important function of the parent as a partner is to share with the program staff information about the child's behavior in the home. It is important, particularly at the onset of the program, for the teaching staff to be aware of the child's likes, dislikes, interests, skills, and weaknesses. Parent expectations should be considered in formulating goals for the child in order to avoid a wide discrepancy between activities at home and at school. Parents should be viewed as the child's first and most important teachers. It is only through their support and their work with the program that progress will be made. Decision-making on goals and intervention strategies should be a mutual process between parents and school.

Parental activities may range from service as an advisory board member, volunteer, or teacher aide to service as an advocate of more support for expanded preschool services in the community. Parents may contribute to the classroom program by making materials, accompanying children on field trips, riding the bus, providing transportation, or sharing interests or skills with children.

A Model for Parent Participation—Unistaps Project

The UNISTAPS Model (an HCEEP project) for parent participation is an interactional-intervention model. The program for each parent, as outlined in the model, evolves out of parents' interests and needs and provides a unique opportunity for a dynamic process of learning. Below is an overview of the model designed by the Family Program Adviser at the Family Oriented Infant/Preschool (ages zero to four and five) Special Education Program in the Minneapolis Public Schools—UNISTAPS Project (Fowler, 1974).

Figure 9

Parents and Staff Jointly Participate in:

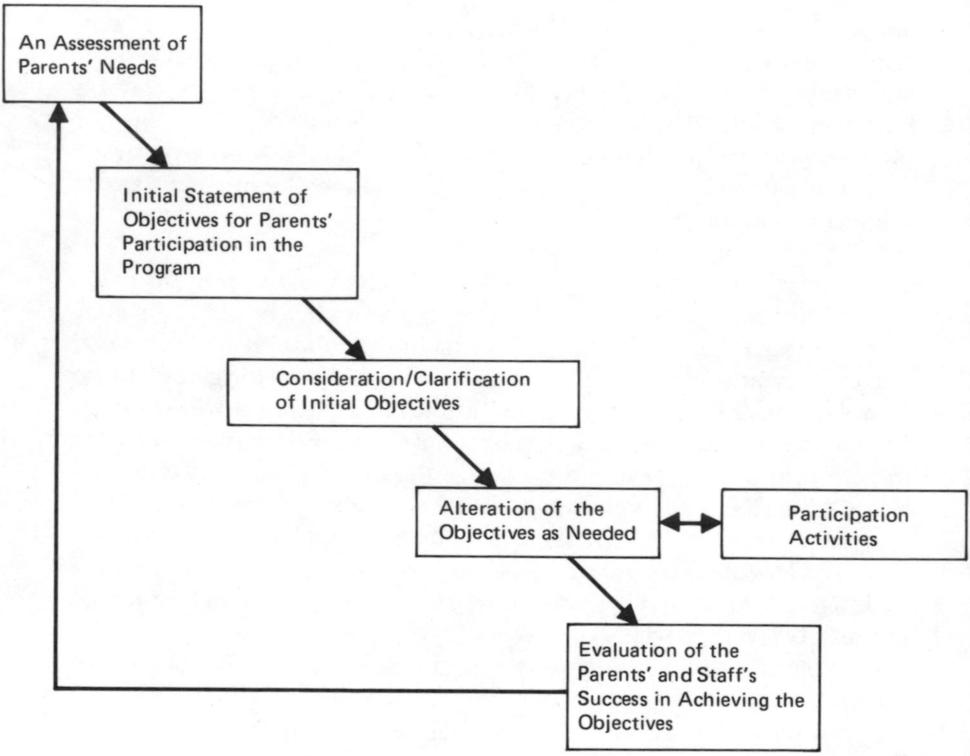

An Assessment of Parents' Needs

Initial Statement of Objectives for Parents' Participation in the Program

Consideration/Clarification of Initial Objectives

Alteration of the Objectives as Needed ←→ Participation Activities

Evaluation of the Parents' and Staff's Success in Achieving the Objectives

Assessment of Parents' Needs.   A professional's direct observation is probably the most reliable way to assess the current level of a parent's knowledge and unmet needs. Information may be obtained during individual parent interviews, parent-group meetings, parent-planning sessions, and through evaluations.

A weekly developmental log is useful if the notations are made in it after the parent has left an individual-parent interview, parent-group meeting, or planning session. The teacher can ask herself such questions as: How does a parent communicate with the child, and how does the child respond? How does the child act around the parent? If both parents were present, did they seem to support each other's questions, expand each other's observations? Did they respond to direct questions by the teacher? What topics were brought up by the parents? What was their general mood? To what extent do they participate in group meetings and meet individual appointments?

The teacher may want to fill out a parent information form or have the parent fill out a needs-assessment questionnaire during one of these sessions. Parents with the assistance of staff should be involved in realistically expressing their own needs.

Initial Statement of Objective/Participation.   Objectives are determined by information gained during the needs assessment. The objectives focus on activities in one of three major categories: education and training, participation, and coordination with services from other agencies. Below are the major content areas within each category.

Education-Training (focusing on family, parents)
Family Workshops (content/skill/overall value)
Parent Information (factual knowledge)
Parental Teaching Style
Early Child Development Series
Behavior Problem Solving Series
Community Parent Education Courses
Integrated Nursery School Observation
Parent Assessment/Child

Participation (cooperative efforts of parent/teacher/staff in working with
    child)
Parent/Teacher Sessions at Home/Preschool Program
Mother/Child Nursery Sessions
Diagnostic Sessions
Prekindergarten Nursery Sessions (Center-based)
General Neighborhood Nursery Sessions
Parent Assessment/Child

Coordination (assisting parents in services from other agencies)
Parent Education Program, Generic Agencies
Information (medical, education)
Referral Assistance
Interagency Educational Planning

Consideration/Clarification.   In this phase the program staff and parents jointly plan the nine-month parent-education program on the basis of jointly determined objectives. The assumption is that increased involvement is useful in parental development of a successful identity, including a feeling of personal worth. A successful identity is a prerequisite for assurance of a stimulating home environment for young children. The parent's realization that they learn from each other as well as from a professional staff generally leads to their increased involvement in the group as the year progresses.

Altered Plan.   A parent-participation plan is altered on the basis of input from both parents and staff. Often, information from the evaluation phase shows that a particular objective is not appropriate. Conditions, and circumstances within the family and home, may change to the extent that plans have to be altered. This phase provides both parents and staff with a feeling that they are not locked into a plan and that a great deal of flexibility exists.

Participation Activities.   Activities are selected from nine major program components based on the needs of individual parents.

Parent Meetings: Mornings, Weekly
Parent Meetings: Evening, Monthly
Integrated Nursery Observation: Periodic
Parents' Initiated Activities: as Needed
Informal Parent Group: Weekly
Family Workshops: Saturday, Monthly
Home or Agency Visit: Periodic
Learning Experiences, Individual / Group Sessions: Weekly, as
     Needed
Home and Agency Services Coordinated: as Needed

The content focus of each component varies with the individual or the group of parents involved. Parents may participate in one or more of the components.

Evaluation.   Evaluation is ongoing in this process. Procedures have been determined for evaluating each parent-participation objective. Evaluation is vital in terms of assessing parents' needs, altering the objectives for parents, and ascertaining the appropriateness and effectiveness of the objectives and activities.

Conclusions

In summary, a program of parent participation requires a team effort. The developers of the program must be familiar with community resources for referral of problems which lie outside the scope of the educational team to solve. Parental growth is best encouraged in a familiar school atmosphere which includes staff members who are trusting and trustworthy. Implementation of a family-oriented preschool program which regards all parents as partners offers the promise of enabling a young child to find satisfaction in daily living and thereby fulfill his parents' realistic expectations.

Bibliography

Calvert, D. R., Olshin, G. M., DeWeerd, M. J. & Berson, M. P. "Office of Education Describes Model Projects for Young Handicapped Children." *Exceptional Child*, 1969, 36, 229–248.

Cohen, E. S. Teaching and Guidance of Preschool Deaf Children. *Proceedings of the International Congress on Education of the Deaf*, 1964, 842–847.

Dreikurs, R. *Children, the Challenge*. New York: Meredith Press, 1964.

Erikson, E. *Childhood and Society* (2nd ed.). New York: Norton, 1963.

Fowler, S. A. "Parenting Children with Special Needs." Unpublished paper presented at the National Convention of the Alexander Graham Bell Association for the Deaf in Atlanta, 1974.

Northcott, W. H. Candidate for Integration: a Hearing-Impaired Child in a Regular Nursery School. *Young Children*, 1970, 25, 367–380.

Northcott, W. H., Nelson, N. V., & Fowler, S. A. "UNISTAPS: A Family-Oriented Infant/Preschool Program for Hearing Impaired Children and Their Parents." *Peabody Journal of Education*, 1974, 51, 192–196.

Weinstein, G. W. "Nursery School With a Difference." *Parents*, 1968, 43, 66–69.

Facilitating Positive Parent-Child Interactions

Audrey Simmons-Martin

To facilitate positive parent-child interactions, an early-childhood program must provide an opportunity for parents to learn about: (1) approaches to child-rearing; (2) ways to use ordinary elements in the child's environment as teaching tools and how to turn everyday experiences into learning experiences; (3) ways to encourage the children's language growth; (4) ways to promote social and emotional development; and (5) ways to find and use various resources in the community. A program must provide these opportunities since parents are their children's first and most influential teachers.

Parent-Professional Planning

Because of expanding professional roles and more learning opportunities for parents, parent involvement in child development programs is no longer limited to providing or receiving information. Today programs aim toward increasing the parents' understanding at many levels of developmental learning and through many kinds of experiences so that they develop greater competence in dealing with their children. Of course, these goals must be applied realistically. Since programs may not be able to bring about drastic changes in the personality of a parent or in child-care practices which have their roots not only in individual knowledge but also in

AUDREY SIMMONS-MARTIN is Director of Early Education at the Central Institute for the Deaf in St. Louis. Her major contributions have been in the areas of language development and parent involvement.

the parent's upbringing, professionals must provide the opportunity for parents to gain greater skill in child-parent interactions. In order to alter some of their own practices, parents need greater understanding of their child's developmental problems, themselves, their family, and community relations.

While each program will strive to achieve its own objectives, professionals should focus upon assisting and supporting the mother in her role as "teacher" of her child. The professional who assumes that responsibility takes on a variety of roles which are dependent on each parent's needs. For example, the professional can be at any one time: (1) a reinforcer supporting everything good the mother does; (2) an activity director giving ideas to the mother who is unsure of what to do; (3) a teacher acting directly and specifically in teaching and demonstrating model activities; and (4) an information seeker and giver sharing information about the child's growth, development, toys, and activities in an incidental way (Nielson & Jeff, 1972).

In the case of a handicapped child, the greatest need from the beginning is parents who can understand the child's problems and adjust to them. He needs parents who, as a result of this understanding, foresee what his needs will be.

The mother's ability to cope with the problems of hour-to-hour and day-to-day child management may require professional attention. Too often, it is assumed that parents need to be taught language stimulation techniques, didactic exercises, etc., rather than being given general suggestions for working with the child through the day.

Parents Mold Children; Children Mold Parents

Most research on parent-child interaction assumes that there is a direct and discernible relation between the parents' behavior, attitudes, and personalities and the child's behavior and personality. This might well be an oversimplification. It may be that the parents and children influence each other in a two-way fashion. Normal children by the age of three months seem to have a very strong control over their parents. It has been said that the mother is a puppet to her three-month-old puppeteer.

Rheingold and Bayley (1964) listed the mother's home activities recorded in a normal environment in order of magnitude as "holds, talks, talks to, feeds, and, looks at face"; as contrasted with those performed in an institution which were "holds, feeds, looks at face, and talks to." It becomes readily apparent that children with special needs present unique problems. For example, if the handicap is a hearing or language impairment, the second and third activities of the mother might soon be extinguished. This is probably because she receives little or no encouragement from the deaf infant. He may not coo, smile, or do any of the reinforcing stunts that the mother needs. Many parents have not had the necessary training for specific types of infant stimulation.

Evidence is accumulating that parenting can be taught and that it is not solely instinctive. From experiments with animals it has been demonstrated that offspring denied "mothering" in their infancy developed maternal behavior themselves that was completely abnormal, ranging from indifference to outright abuse. The "mothering" behavior of those primates entrusted to wire surrogate mothers was inferior to those provided with cloth surrogates, but both were poorer mothers than primates who had had their real mothers (Harlow and Harlow, 1962).

It is readily apparent that if a child has a speech or hearing problem there is some degree of breakdown in communication. This breakdown can lead to difficulties in interpersonal relationships which can lead to further breakdowns in communication. The parent contributes to the child's problems and vice versa.

A Parent-Child Program—Its Goals and Activities

The primary goal of a parent-child program at the preschool level is to enable the child to achieve the maximum level of his abilities. The literature is replete with evidence of the parents' role, in particular the mother's role, in determining the child's achievement as an adult. Earl S. Schaefer (1972) presents a good review of recent research in this area. The preschool years are widely acknowledged to be the most crucial years in the child's total development. If this is so for the "normal" child, it is all the more so for a handicapped child. Thus, the parent of a handicapped child must deal not only with his own feelings about the child's handicap, but also with the needs of the growing child who happens to be handicapped. The parent, during the child's preschool years not only seeks resolution of guilt feelings and of the *why* questions—"Why me?" "Why my child?"—but also seeks direction in meeting the needs of the child represented by the questions—"What do I do" "How do I do it?"

With the primary purpose of a parent-child program at the preschool level in mind, the goals and activities may be grouped into three categories: immediate, intermediate, and long-range. The immediate goals and activities may be viewed as the gates or doors which provide access to the intermediate ones which in turn lead to the long-range. These three categories of goals and activities are presented in Figure 10 (see pages 80–81).

The Role of the Professional

Because of this range of goals and activities, as well as the variety of situations and needs presented by the parents and their child, professionals must assume a variety of roles. These roles include: (1) listener—many parents have no one else to whom they can talk about their concerns for their child, (2) enabler—the teacher through her activities enables the parents to achieve their own maximal functioning as parents, (3) model—through the teacher's interactions and activities with the child she provides the parents a role or roles to imitate, (4) reality tester—the parents often need a person outside the family to help them test the reality of a situation as it concerns themselves or their child, (5) integrator—the teacher enables the parents to pull the bits and pieces into a meaningful whole, (6) interpreter—the teacher puts professional jargon into language the parents can understand, (7) resource person—the parents have one person to check out such things as new information and new programs as they relate to their child, and last but not least, (8) teacher.

Individualizing Parent Involvement

It is vital for an early childhood program to get parents involved on an individual basis. At Central Institute for the Deaf, the parents originally came together to get the best information they could about their children's hearing problems, and to learn what they could expect of their children and how to deal with their handicaps. Soon it became clear that they needed more. They had needs themselves, as parents; they had their own attitudes, feelings, and expectations; they had goal-setting problems. They needed to focus on their roles as shapers of their children's behavior, particularly language behavior.

With young babies, parents may have difficulty in participating in teaching-learning situations. The only effective way to "teach" is to adopt a natural approach. All parents have many opportunities in their homes, moment-by-moment, for shaping linguistic and cognitive behavior; e.g., dressing, washing, feeding, playing. However, parents need help in translating what they are told to do into actually doing it in their own homes. Therefore a Home Demonstration Center, which is a real home in appearance, was established. It is an old house with two apartments, like the other ones on the block. The apartments are furnished in a simple manner. They are warm, inviting, and comfortable. The first floor apartment has a living room, dining room, kitchen and bedroom. On the second floor is a kitchen, a living-dining room, a bedroom, a child's room, and a bath. All appliances work with some degree of regularity. The refrigerators, while not laden, are reasonably full, as are the cabinets and closets. In short, nothing is contrived. There are no offices, nor office or school paraphernalia around; these are in the Institute itself, a close half-block away. In this setting, the program seeks to facilitate positive parent-child interactions. It is here that the parent and child come for an hourly session with a teacher of the deaf. During this time, she attempts to help them learn to seize every opportunity for language input. Since the center's emphasis is on helping first-rate parents to develop and not on creating second-rate classroom teachers, only experiences that each mother would be having in her particular home are used.

In her own home the parent is the teacher in the broadest sense of the term. Therefore, in our Home Demonstration Center she demonstrates how well she is progressing while the real teacher makes appropriate comments. It is obvious that the latter has to be skilled in creating an atmosphere of ease, transforming apprehensiveness into creative energy, and helping the parents feel the need for interaction with their child.

Because the Center does not want the children to grow up unstimulated in well-furnished pleasant rooms filled with a variety of expensive, meaningless toys, as is sometimes the case, its program personnel try to provide basic perceptual, sensory, and other cognitive experiences. Through his perception, the child develops appropriate concepts and vocabulary associated with experiences which have features in common. Mediated with similar language, the concept develops and the language is absorbed. In this way, the child receives the data with which to learn the rules. For example, "washing" is a concept which has linguistic form: wash hands, wash face, hair, wash someone else's face, hands, etc., wash dishes, pots, pans, silver, wash clothes, wash the car, wash the dog, wash the windows, wash the floor, etc. The implements are soap, sponge, washcloth, mop. The features in common are water, soap, and rubbing action, but the most important common feature is the word "wash." It is hypothesized that the word "wash" can be

Figure 10

Three Categories of Goals and Activities

LONG-RANGE GOALS AND ACTIVITIES

Child's maximal achievement
of his inate abilities

INTERMEDIATE GOALS AND ACTIVITIES

● Modify the child's environment to minimize those attitudes or
behaviors of parents or siblings which could impede the child's
opportunity for development

● Help parents in setting and resetting realistic targets for achievement
in their child

● Assist parents in providing a stimulating home environment for
promoting total growth in their child

● Assist the parents in selecting the type of education which gives the
child optimum opportunity for development

IMMEDIATE GOALS AND ACTIVITIES

- Listen to the parents

- Deal with the parent's feelings

- Provide emotional support to the parents

- Determine the extent of the parents' background knowledge

- Provide information to the parents in a way that they can understand

- Help the parents become thoroughly familiar with the facts and implications of their child's problems as they become known

- Assist the parents to achieve consistently firm, but affectionate, handling of the child in a variety of situations

- Strengthen the positive aspects of parent–child interaction

- Help the parents learn to be sensitive to natural and informal situations in everyday life which make language more readily meaningful to the child

- Teach the parents to be alert to ideal opportunities, not only for the development of communication skills, but also the total, integrated development of the child

- Provide parents with information about available resources

learned more readily when experienced in a variety of situations rather than when experienced many times in only one situation. There is some interesting data available which confirm this hypothesis. (Kol'tsovs, 1962)

The appropriateness of the activity is part of the Center's direction. (We have even had doubts about such things as storing our milk in a jar since most children use a carton.) Part of this is discussed with the mother prior to her demonstration with her child of the task or tasks she has planned for the hour.

Frequently advice on good "mothering" is given. Certainly good mothering techniques are reinforced. When she does something to get her child involved, captures some of his language output, or anticipates his needs, staff members reinforce her with praise. Sometimes the teacher helps the mother with the toilet training, feeding, bathing, and even clothing.

Family Conferences

Siblings of the young child should be encouraged to come with mother whenever possible to the family conferences. While this may create havoc for the professional, this, after all, is the true situation that faces the mother at her home. Program personnel strive also to have contacts with the father as well as the mother. As noted earlier, the presence of a handicapped child is likely to intensify family stresses. It may, for example, decrease communication between the parents who may have developed very different views of the child. If professionals can set a pattern of forthright discussion about what the child has done, can do, might do, and will do, the parents' attention and discussion may be focused into meaningful channels.

The teacher never assumes that a conference in which the parents nod their heads in apparent assent necessarily represents real understanding. The intense emotional bond between parents and child may preclude rapid attitudinal change. Genuine change is a time-dependent phenomenon resulting from continuous exposure of the parents to reality-oriented situations. In these sessions with the teachers, parents are encouraged to be themselves and to disclose their own thoughts and feelings. As Beasley stated,

> to the extent that parents themselves are granted acceptance and respect, they will be more free to give this to their child. . . . Since the problems of a child in language and speech originate and exist in an interpersonal setting, modifications of this environment may be highly important if change is to take place [Beasley, 1956, p. 319].

Group Education

Fundamental to the parents' understanding of the total child is their knowledge of certain key areas of learning behavior. For this reason the program of parent groups continues as an essential part of the Institute's services. In these programs, language development, hearing aids, behavior modification, genetics, and hearing are discussed. Some of the speakers have been deaf adults, the director and the principal of Central Institute, child psychologists, and other parents.

Before thinking about what parents gain from experience in groups, a question must be asked. What is it that they really need? There are some universal trends that have been observed. For example, parents want up-to-date and accurate information that they can understand regarding their children's development. Parents also want to have practical information about what they can do to help their child develop to his greatest capacity, and what they may expect that capacity to be. In other words, they want to know how to manage now and what they have to look forward to.

These are the questions parents often bring first to professional people, with a very strong sense of urgency. It is only later that they reveal that they need to know more about themselves, about their own widely conflicting, but normal, feelings, and their own special level of tolerance for the demands that are put upon them. They need to have help in recognizing both where they are weak and where they are strong so that they can turn to appropriate sources for help when necessary. They also want to know the effects that a handicapped child can have on the family as a whole—the strain that this places on the marriage and the effects on the other children in the family.

Surely some of the information parents need can be made available to them through the printed word and in lectures at large meetings. Yet these "formal presentations" have their limitations. Parents will take from such reading and talks only what they are able to take from them, and they may react to this material in ways that one cannot predict in advance.

Finally, professionals must not underestimate the impact of one parent upon other parents in these group situations. The Institute's mothers' group meetings range from small to large. One group is for the beginning mothers, another for the continuing mothers. A third group is a combination of the two. These all meet once a month. It should be noted that the parents proceed very quickly to enter into significant discussions, and a rather immediate sense of identification takes place among the parents.

Summary

In summary, there has been a change in emphasis in programs for parents from didactic course work to total involvement. This involvement has shifted from parent becoming an instructor to parent being a teacher in the broad sense. Knowledge related to the handicap is still essential, but parents need help in parenting. They need to recognize the opportunities available in the home and the impact of their child on them and their family. Professionals need to be alert to the range of emotional periods through which parents pass. They must accept parents for themselves and move from there. Group opportunities for emotional support and exchange should also not be neglected.

Bibliography

Beasley, J. "Relationship of Parental Attitudes to Development of Speech Problems." *Journal of Speech and Hearing Disorders,* 1956, *21,* 317–321.

Bowlby, J. "The Nature of a Child's Tie to His Mother." *International Journal of Psychology,* 1958, *39,* 350–373.

Elliott, L., & Armbruster, V. "Some Possible Effects of the Delay of Early Treatment of Deafness." *Journal of Speech and Hearing Research,* 1967, *10,* 209–224.

Farber, B. "Effects of Severely Mentally Retarded Child on the Family." In Trapp & Hamelstein (Eds.), *Readings on the Exceptional Child.* New York: Appleton-Century-Crofts, 1962.

Harlow, H., & Harlow, M. "Social Deprivation in Monkeys." *Scientific American,* 1962, *207,* 2–10.

Kol'tsovs, N. M. "The Formation of Higher Nervous Activity of the Child." *Psychological Review,* 1962, *69,* 344–354.

Lowell, E. "Parental Skills and Attitudes, Including Home Training." *The Young Deaf Child: Identification and Management,* Supplement No. 206. Stockholm: Acta-Oto-Laryngologica, 1965.

Michaels, J., & Shucman, H. "Observations on the Psychodynamics of Parents of Retarded Children." *American Journal of Mental Deficiency,* 1962, *66,* 568–573.

Neilson, T. G., & Jeffs, M. G. "Video Tape Documentation of an Infant Education Program." *Audiovisual Instruction,* 1972, *17,* 27–29.

Rheingold, H. & Bayley, N. "The Later Effects of an Experimental Modification of Mothering." In Stendler (Ed.), *Readings in Child Behavior & Development.* New York: Harcourt, Brace, & World, 1964.

Schaefer, E. S. "Parents as Educators: Evidence from Cross-Sectional, Longitudinal, and Intervention Research." In W. W. Hartup (Ed.), *The Young Child,* (Vol. 2). Washington, D.C.: National Association for the Education of Young Children, 1972.

Shontz, F. "Reactions to Crisis." *Volta Review*, 1965, *67*, 364–370.
Wolpe, Z. "Play Therapy, Psychodrama, and Parent Counseling." In L. Travis (Ed.), *Handbook of Speech Pathology*. New York: Appleton, 1957.

Part

The Operation of Parent
Programs:
Four Perspectives

A Center-Based Parent-Training Model

Alice H. Hayden

The experimental Education Unit School, in the Child Development and Mental Retardation Center (CDMRC) at the University of Washington, provides instructional programs for handicapped children from birth to eighteen years of age. This chapter will focus on the service aspects of the programs in the Unit's Model Preschool Center for Handicapped Children which is funded in part by the U.S. Office of Education, Bureau of Education for the Handicapped (under P.L. 91-230, Part C). The school not only provides instruction for children, but also serves as a demonstration-training facility for university students from many different disciplines, for paraprofessionals in different fields, and for parents who are trained at school to work with their own children at home. Each of the five classrooms for preschool age children serves two groups of children a day; the children are grouped into classes according to age and to the severity of their handicaps.

Because the children spend only two or three hours per day at school, it is essential that parents learn how to help their children develop self-help, motor, communication, cognitive and social skills in the home, where the children spend so much of their time. The different types of parent training and involvement depend upon the particular program the child is in and upon his and his parents' or

ALICE H. HAYDEN is Director of the Model Preschool Center for Handicapped Children (Experimental Education Unit) at the Child Development and Mental Retardation Center at the University of Washington in Seattle. Her interests include: Down's syndrome, the improvement of instruction for young children, the systematic observation of young children, and the evaluation of programs for young children.

family's special needs. The focus is always on the child, and on how the staff and the parents can best work together to meet his needs. Those who are working with parents need to recognize that parents' needs are as different and as individual as those of their children.

Parents usually find that, among the many advantages of being trained in the Center, rather than at home, is the opportunity to talk to and work with other parents of handicapped children. Those parents who have children with similar handicapping conditions often develop strong bonds of friendship and are appreciative of the gains made by all the children.

At the Model Preschool Center we do not have a "parent training package." There are several reasons for this. First, our emphasis is on individualized instruction for every child, and that emphasis extends to staff and parent training as well. Although there are basic principles underlying the training given everyone at the Center, we believe that individual parents and families, like their children, have unique needs and problems, and that to be effective in meeting these individual needs, we must maintain flexible training. Second, our center is different from most schools where parents play an active role in that children are referred to us for relatively short-term intervention—most children spend from one academic quarter to two years at the Model Preschool Center before returning to placements in their home communities. Further, the children may arrive at any time during the school year. So it is not possible for us to plan a single program that begins in September and ends in June—too many of our parents would be short-changed by such inflexibility.

The one exception to this general pattern of short-term intervention occurs in our Down's Syndrome programs. Many of the children who participate in these programs are referred to us when they are newborn infants, and they may be entered in our infant learning program as early as two weeks of age. Some of the children in these programs have stayed with us for as long as three years; obviously, their parents have experienced a more typical "parent training program" than most others in terms of continuity and duration.

Intake

Parents may apply directly to the Child Development and Mental Retardation Center for counseling or service, or they may be referred by clinics, agencies, private physicians, nurses, psychologists, or school districts. How the parents get to the Center is not important; what happens after they arrive is. If a child needs help, the staff of the Clinical Training Unit at the Child Development and Mental Retardation Center determine which clinic within the unit or team of representatives from different disciplines can best undertake the information-gathering necessary to learn as much about the child's problems as possible. If a child is not receiving services essential to his development or treatment, recommendations will be made for placing him in an appropriate program. The first consideration is given to the services available in the child's home community—where would he be best served, given his age and his handicapping condition(s)?

In any case, consultations with personnel from the child's home school district are essential inasmuch as the school district is, or will be, responsible for the child's eventual education in a regular or special education program. An objective of the Experimental Education Unit is to return each child to an appropriate placement in his home community as soon as it appears that he will be ready to function adequately in a school district program. The parents must, of course, supply some of the needed information and must also be involved in any decisions about placement. Parents may be invited to visit various appropriate programs, to talk with their personnel, and to observe the children enrolled. Practical considerations such as transportation must, of course, be taken into account.

When a child is being considered for placement in the Model Preschool Center the admissions coordinator informs parents of the opportunities for parent involvement and participation in Model Preschool Center programs, and frequently introduces them to another parent whose child has been enrolled for a while. The parents are invited to visit the program their child will be placed in and to meet the staff if they have not already done so. If the parents are expected to participate in one or more class sessions each week, they are informed of this before the child is admitted, and a time schedule is worked out which will be most convenient for them. Parents are told about the regular parent-staff meetings, usually held at least once a month and in the evening so that both parents can attend. There are also all-school parent-teacher meetings each quarter. In addition the admissions officer explains parent consent forms and clearances, available insurance policies, and services which may be provided through the university hospital at a very modest fee.

When it appears that a child is a candidate for placement in one of the model preschool programs, his needs are discussed at a meeting of the consultant advisory committee. Meetings of this committee are scheduled once or twice a month, depending upon the number of children to be considered for placement. Prior to the meeting, the child's records are reviewed to make certain that all relevant information as well as parental consent and clearance forms are in. Program coordinators or head teachers in the different programs discuss how the child's needs can best be met, what support help is needed, and what arrangements have been made to obtain it. The latter arrangements are usually made by the school nurse consultant. The admissions coordinator may also report on the information that has been exchanged with the school district in which the parents live, arrangements for transporting the child, and the date when the child will begin his work at the unit. Every effort is made to keep the time required for admission procedures as short as possible. If it appears that there may be a delay in placing the child in a program at the Model Preschool because of a lack of openings, alternative placements are considered. If a child has to wait until his name comes up on a "waiting list," services that he badly needs can be delayed. For this reason, our "waiting list" is short, and we act to place children in a program as quickly as possible if one of our programs is considered by the referring agency and the Clinical Training Unit to be the most appropriate or only possible placement for a given child.

Parents have the opportunity to ask any questions they may have. A well-informed parent who is involved in the parent-training programs is a good public relations person and can be very helpful to other parents of handicapped children in the community. By the time a child is admitted to a program in the Model Preschool Center, the parent is usually eager for information and the assistance which can be provided by the staff. The parent may have collected information about the child's behavior at home which can be very helpful to the staff in initiating his program at the Unit.

For instance, children may have certain annoying or puzzling behavior patterns, or problems which are of great concern to their parents or the family. To give just one example of the ways in which parents and staff work together to remediate such problems, parents having children enrolled in any of the Down's Syndrome programs are asked to list home management goals for their children. The staff then helps in the statement of specific objectives and in determining procedures for the attainment of these goals. The evaluation of progress is ongoing and integral to this process. Goals for home management are indicated on a form such as that shown in Figure 11.

Figure 11
Goals for Home Management

Dear Parent:

Please indicate one or two objectives in any of the following areas that you would like your child to attain this quarter. Be specific. After you have identified these objectives, we will discuss them with you and will help you plan a program or programs to meet them.

(Please state objectives in terms of child behaviors.)

Gross Motor

1. _____

2. _____

Fine Motor

1. _____

2. _____

Self–help Skills

1. _____

2. _____

Preacademic Skills

1. _____

2. _____

Social Interaction and Language

1. _____

2. _____

Behaviors you would like to increase or decrease

1. _____

2. _____

Please return this form during the first week of school. Thank you.

Sincerely yours,
Val Dmitriev
Coordinator, Down's Syndrome Programs

If a child exhibits behaviors that are annoying, the parent may think that the child engages in these behaviors "all the time." At the Center, the staff members try to get the parent to collect information on the actual frequency of these behaviors and to encourage the parent to reinforce the child for his desirable behaviors or approximations to desirable behaviors. Helping the parent realize that the child does some things that please him is an important function of the data collection. No child is "bad" all the time or "good" all the time. Staff and parents can work together to increase the frequency of desirable behaviors and to decrease the frequency of the annoying behaviors.

Delivery of Services

We start with parent-training as soon as possible after a child's handicapping condition has been identified. Acceptance of the fact that a child has a handicap is not easy for most parents. While they are going through this period of adjustment the parents usually discover that there are sources of help and that they, the parents and family, have contributions to make that will help the child. In the past, many parents have said that the most difficult time they had with their handicapped child was between the time the pediatrician no longer worked with them on a regular basis and the time the child entered some type of school program. During this period the parents did not know what they could "do" for their child; thus, they waited and felt useless. The situation is greatly changed today with the many and increasing numbers of preschool programs now available for infants and young children. In these, parents can and do play active roles, thereby decreasing their frustrations.

Support to parents and families while they are recognizing and accepting the fact that they have a child with a handicapping condition must be provided so that the parents do not dwell too much on being burdened and on the questions raised in their own minds and by their relatives or neighbors. There are misconceptions about many types of handicapped children; these misconceptions may cause parents to be embarrassed, to have guilt feelings, and to despair. Parents frequently have questions they are afraid to ask or that they do not know how to ask. The sooner some of their questions are answered objectively and their misconceptions are dispelled, the better it is for all concerned.

Those professionals and paraprofessionals working with parents must keep in mind that the needs of parents and families are as unique and different as those of individual handicapped children. It sometimes takes some "extrasensitive" perception to assess the stated or implied concerns of the parents and to get the parents to feel free to express these. Some parents hesitate to talk about problems related to their having a handicapped child, such as marital difficulties, financial problems, or the well-intentioned but not very helpful comments and suggestions of relatives and friends. To reiterate, some families need a time for adjustment, a time to recognize that they need help; and they need encouragement to seek the assistance that is available.

Perhaps excerpts from two recent publications will express the initial impact on parents of being told at their child's birth that the child is handicapped. In the first example, a minister shares with his congregation the reaction he and his wife experienced.

> Three of the saddest words in the English language are "we had hoped . . ." They capture some of the deepest pain, loss and disillusionment human beings can feel. . . .
>
> . . . Todd finally arrived at 7:30 P.M., five weeks premature and weighing in at 4½ pounds. We were very apprehensive about Todd's progress Saturday, since the first 24 hours are a crucial time for premature infants . . . Then we learned Saturday night that Todd's prematurity was one of our smaller worries. We were told that Todd has Down's syndrome. . . .
>
> We don't see ourselves as unusual or exclusive. We think our experience is representative of the process other parents have gone through in this kind of situation.
>
> Some of you know what it's like to look forward to the birth of your first child with eagerness and anticipation, a child with whom to share your world and your life, and then be told after the birth that your hopes and expectations have just been shattered by some chromosomal accident. It is a grief process because there is real grief over the loss of the child you expected and grief over the devastation of your dreams and hopes. . . .
>
> There were times when we didn't want to believe this was happening to us—times when, as one of our prayers of confession put it, we wanted to "hold out for better terms." We could hardly hear, much less speak, the words *mental retardation*. We felt almost overwhelmed, and the future looked very bleak and uncompromising. (Martz, 1974, pp. 34–35)

Another reaction is expressed by the parent of a child in the Down's Syndrome program in the Model Preschool Center for Handicapped Children. The child was admitted to our program when she was five weeks old.

When Angie . . . was born 2½ years ago, her mother's reaction was hysteria. Angie was, the doctor said, a mongoloid.

"I had never even been near a retarded person before," her mother said. "I thought, 'Oh, my God, what did I do during this pregnancy that caused this?' "

Angie's parents are long since over their shock. "Pretty soon you just have to get busy," Angie's mother said. . . .

She often is asked to visit new mothers of Down's children in the hospital. . . .

"To be told is devastating, and all the books on it paint such a bleak picture. It's natural to be scared, afraid of pitying the child. We all have a fleeting wish that the child will die. It's a normal, healthy reaction. It's fear of the unknown." (Mills, 1974, pp. 8-10)

From these two examples of parents' reactions to having a handicapped child, it should be immediately apparent that professionals who are going to work with such parents must start "where the parents are" and must not contribute to the feelings they already have of being overwhelmed. Certainly the professionals will be acutely aware of many things that need to be done for the child. However, the families may be more upset by specific concerns that seem paramount to them—concern about the child's feeding, the possibilities of his having other, associated conditions, and their own perceived inability to cope with what they consider to be problems in the day-to-day care of the child in the home.

Indeed, there may be many things parents need to know, but let's start with what they perceive to be their needs and let them discover other ways we can work together as partners. No professional team, no matter how expert, can meet all of the child's or parents' needs at the same time. We who are concerned with child instruction often talk about the child's readiness for certain types of activities. Suppose we also think of "parent readiness" for coping with different problems.

In a multidisciplinary center-school, there are opportunities to work with parents and families of handicapped children in a number of different ways. If we are fortunate enough to be able to work with the child and family soon after the handicapping condition has been identified, we can relieve many parental anxieties and start focusing on the child's problem(s) in those early, crucial months and years of the child's life. Early identification and intervention can prevent many other conditions which compound the child's difficulties. It is easier to start applying procedures that are effective in dealing with certain types of behaviors than it is to have to correct ineffective methods of coping with problems. Frequently, the first step in parent training is to convince the parent of the importance of becoming involved in an early training program. Well-intentioned people may have tried to allay parents' anxieties by suggesting that perhaps the child will "grow out of it." Such suggestions frequently do more harm than good and in most cases they do not allay the parents' concerns. The parents still recognize that "something is wrong" and that they need help in finding out what that something is and what they can do about it. Such suggestions often delay the parents' search for help.

Procedures

Some common procedures are used throughout the Model Preschool Center for Handicapped Children, and parents learn how to use many of them. The procedures derive from the basic principles of behavior modification: initial assessment of child needs, ongoing assessment and systematic observation, daily measurement of pupil progress, modification of individual programs when data indicate that a child's particular program is not resulting in the expected progress. Data is kept on at least two behaviors at a time for each child; in many cases, particularly where parent or volunteer help is available, data is kept on additional behaviors.

Infant Programs. In working with infants from birth to eighteen months we try to assess the child's needs and the parents' specific concerns. In some cases, we seek assistance from physical therapists, nutritionists, social workers, and other representatives of different disciplines who may be able to provide help and instruction to the individual parent or to groups of parents who have common needs and problems such as feeding children or developing their muscle tone. Normally, the parent will bring the child to the Model Preschool Center at least one day a week. Each parent and child pair receives thirty minutes of individual attention during which the parent is shown how to stimulate the child, to help him to attend to sounds or objects, and to make eye contact with adults. The child's responses are reinforced, as are the parents'. Parents frequently stay on after their session to watch our work with other children and their parents so that they may learn through observation either in the classroom or from an observation booth. We encourage parents to report on the progress of the child at home and to ask any questions they may have. They are invited to call staff members at the school or at home whenever they have questions or special concerns. We want the parents to feel that help is as close as their telephone.

Professionalism must be coupled with humanism in helping parents cope with their needs and the child's needs in these early weeks and months when much support is needed. A parent-training class is not the answer to parents' needs for assistance at this point. A class could not move fast enough, and the instructor could not anticipate the needs of a group of parents and plan a program that would accommodate them.

Early Preschool Programs   Children from nineteen months to three years of age participate in early preschool programs. Such preschool programs may last for two hours or more and may be conducted four or five days a week. The daily schedule provides a variety of activities designed to develop self-help, motor, communication, social and cognitive skills. In some programs, the parents work with the staff right in the classroom, and each parent has an opportunity to participate in the program at least one day per week. In other programs, the parent observes the work being done in the classroom and has an opportunity to meet with a staff member to discuss the child's progress and to ask questions about working with the child in the home. Data is collected on child progress in every session of every program. Videotapes offer an opportunity to staff and parents alike to review the work done and the children's responses. Every class session is followed by a staff meeting to which parents are invited if they have participated in that class session. Pupil progress is noted and plans are made for the next day's session.

When children and parents have special needs, special classes may be offered. For instance, parents of deaf children may attend classes to learn English sign language and finger spelling while the children are being taught such skills in the classroom, so that the parents can make use of every opportunity which may help the child acquire language and speech skills.

While the emphasis in this chapter is on the earliest preschool years here at the Center, it should also be noted that the procedures described here are used in the Advanced Preschool, Kindergarten, and Pre-Primary classes at the Center and in all of the Center's field programs. Ours is a demonstration center, offering outreach and technical assistance to a wide variety of field programs; because parent involvement is integral to all programs here at the Center, it is one program component that is heavily emphasized in field programs, too.

Parent Participation in Procedures Common to All Programs.   In every program, the staff members work with parents in many different ways. There are numerous parent conferences, parent group meetings, direct parent participation, individual parent instruction, and group parent instruction. Parent groups are instructed in the steps of normal child development in the areas of self-help, gross and fine motor, communication, social and cognitive skills. Emphasis is placed on the parent's understanding of normal development because one of the goals of the Model Preschool is to bring each child's development as close to the norms as possible. However, care is taken to point out the wide range within normal development. Parents learn, through observing and charting children's progress in these different areas, that children progress at different rates in developing skills. For instance, a child may develop normally in motor and social skills but he may show some lag in communication and in cognitive development. Parents are taught how to apply at home the procedures used in school to help their child come closer to the norm, and the parents learn to keep data on the child's performance at home. In this way, the parents of all children are drawn into a cooperative effort with the school staff to bring each child as close to normal skill development as possible.

Liaison and Follow-through

In addition to showing consideration for the individual child and his family and individualizing programs of instruction for both the child and the parents, our staff places emphasis on developing the competence, confidence and independence of the child and his parents. Parents usually feel the need for much supervision at first— they want to be certain that they are "doing the right thing." The staff members reinforce the parents when they have learned what to do. They also make sure that the parent doesn't feel that the child will perform a skill for or respond to the staff member but not the parent. It is frequently necessary to point out—"See, he did it for you, too." The staff member asks the parent to report what the child does at home. Parents' feelings of insecurity and doubt about their abilities to work with their own children must be dispelled as quickly as possible. Demonstrating that their work is effective is the best way to achieve the goal of parental security and independence in working with their own children.

The following condensed excerpts from Model Preschool case studies illustrate the important roles parents can play as data-takers and behavior modifiers. They also are good examples of ways in which parents and staff work together to remediate a particular problem that the parents or family find worrisome. In both cases, the children's names are fictitious.

The first study concerns Randy, a four-year-old boy whose mother was convinced that her son was always naughty and getting into mischief, that no matter what she did he would not change, and furthermore, that his behavior was worse when she was out of the room. Although his teachers at the Model Preschool agreed that a lot of his behavior was inappropriate, they had noticed some improvement at school. His mother, however, had not noticed any change at home. The staff recognized that simply telling Randy's mother that he had some appropriate behaviors would not change her mind; they reasoned that, if she were to collect data herself, she might have a different picture of Randy's behavior and what could be done to change the inappropriate behavior. She eagerly agreed to a program in which she would collect data over a two-hour period each day.

> . . . Based on the mother's verbal descriptions of what went on in the home, a data form was drawn up. The left hand side was labeled negative child behaviors and had four columns in which the parent could enter 1) each occurrence of an inappropriate behavior, 2) what she did when it occurred, 3) the time, and 4) whether or not she was in the same room. The right side of the page was divided into the same four columns but was labeled positive child behavior. . . . She arrived for her next conference armed with several days' records and some preliminary conclusions that she herself had begun to draw from her data. Most noteworthy was the indisputable evidence that Randy was not all bad. . . .
>
> Prior to the next conference, the teacher found a way to code and display the mother's data [to give] almost instant read-out on the dynamics of each two-hour session. . . .
>
> There was concrete corroboration that Randy wasn't all bad; in fact, he was a pretty good boy much of the time; that her being out of the room wasn't necessarily the SD (discriminative stimulus) for his misbehaviors [and] that she really was doing a pretty good job of reinforcing Randy's appropriate behaviors. Further analysis revealed that the bad behaviors often occurred in clusters that did not cover a long time-span but led the mother to the conclusion that Randy was continuously bad; [also] that the mother was inconsistent in handling Randy's inappropriate behaviors: sometimes she scolded, sometimes she spanked, sometimes she ignored, and sometimes she actually rewarded . . . (Allen, 1972, pp. 251–254)

Randy's mother and the staff continued to work together for several weeks—collecting and analyzing data, using these data as a basis for establishing a program to remediate Randy's behavior. The changes in Randy's behavior and in his mother's ability to deal with it were remarkably good.

The next study concerns four and a half-year-old Leslie, whose problem is dawdling—one that almost all parents must cope with at some time or another.

> . . . As most of us who have worked with parents know, telling a parent what to do to remediate a situation rarely has durable efficacy. Instead, the teacher asked the mother to describe, that is, pinpoint, the times when the child's procrastinating annoyed or angered her the most. Not getting herself dressed for school in the morning was a prime annoyance, for this was the time that the mother was most harassed. The next question asked was whether Leslie could in fact dress herself. "Of course she can," answered the mother with exasperation, "if she wants to. She just never wants to."
>
> The teacher asked the mother to jot down the time that she gave Leslie the first cue to get dressed as well as each time she checked on her, scolded, helped her, or interacted with her in any way. The final data point was to be the time that the dressing was finally accomplished by whatever means. . . .
>
> The mother had five additional days of data to present at the next conference. A quick perusal indicated three things: 1) most days it was taking Leslie 30 to 45 minutes to get dressed, 2) mother was supplying 6 to 9 prompts and scoldings each day, and 3) mother usually ended up dressing the child herself. A couple of questions were in order at this point. One had to do with finding out what the mother considered a reasonable dressing time, and the second to find out if Leslie preferred coming to school to staying home. The mother replied she did not care how long Leslie took to dress as long as she was ready before the school cab driver came. Mother also reported that Leslie was really upset whenever she could not come to school. Armed with this information, the teacher made the following suggestions:
>
> 1. Continue taking data.
> 2. Tell Leslie that if she did not get herself dressed in time for her ride, she would have to stay home.
> 3. Reduce to three the number of contacts made during dressing time. If, when she went into the room, Leslie was making even an approximation to dressing, the mother could give her a bit of assistance and much verbal praise for her efforts. If Leslie was doing something other than dressing, the mother was to turn and walk out without saying a word.
> 4. Give Leslie one final warning about 6 or 7 minutes before the arrival of the cab.
>
> The next day Leslie and her mother arrived at school 15 minutes late. Leslie was teary-eyed, her mother obviously upset. It seemed that

Leslie had thrown a super scene over missing her ride and therefore school. She had cried, screamed, pleaded with mother to bring her and mother had finally succumbed. A quick conference with mother followed in which she was counseled that if she really did want to eliminate Leslie's dawdling then she must allow her to experience the negative consequences of dawdling—not getting to come to school—no matter how difficult it might be for the mother for a few days. Within a very few days Leslie was dressing herself much more quickly and continued to do so with only an occasional relapse. (Allen, 1972, pp. 248–250)

Professionals interested in parent training will find an excellent review of procedures such as those applied in our programs in an article entitled, "Using Parents as Change Agents for Their Children: A Review." This article by Claudia A. Johnson and Reger C. Katz (1973) provides an extensive review of the literature on "the use of parents in therapeutic roles [that] has resulted from an explicit technology of behavior modification predicted on the analysis and manipulation of environmental contingencies."

Evaluation

Parents can be and are taught to be reliable data-takers. However, this takes much time and effort on the part of both staff and parents. In our Model Preschool Programs, we spend 500–600 hours a quarter with parents in the many different types of parent involvement described earlier. The total time spent with parents over the course of a full year (four quarters) will range from 2,000 to 2,400 hours. It is time and energy well invested for both staff and parents in terms of pupil progress. If a child is not making the expected progress, we do not ask, "What is wrong with the child?" or "What is wrong with the parent or the trainee?" We ask, "What is wrong with the child's program, and how can we modify it to ensure that the child's progress can proceed at a reasonable rate appropriate for his age level and handicapping condition(s)?" Continuous measurement and analysis of data provide information for improving programs. The use of videotapes and the preparation of case studies also greatly assist in recording and reviewing training and classroom activities. There are also excellent dissemination forms useful in our many field programs where parents play an essential role in replicating our procedures and in improving programs for handicapped children.

What Do Parents Do for Us and for Others Working with Handi-capped Children?   Certainly this chapter would not be complete if it did not include some information about the many ways parents have assisted us in our programs and in furthering other programs for handicapped children and their families. Their contributions take many forms and it is interesting to note that many of the things they do are projects they initiated.

First of all, the parents are helpful in working with children and families who are newly enrolled in our programs. They are enthusiastic about the gains their own children have made and are accepting of and reassuring to the newly enrolled children and their families. They form car pools if necessary to transport children or to come to parent meetings. They bring in items they think will be of interest to other parents or to the children.

They also participate in a Parent to Parent Program, which lets pediatricians know that they are willing to visit and talk with parents who have recently been told that they have a handicapped child. They want other parents to know about the resources that are available to help the child and the family.

Moreover, it was a parent group that was instrumental in working with students from the University of Washington Law School in drafting "Education for All" legislation and in getting support for that legislation. These parents are still interested in seeing that the law is fully implemented and that funds are provided to do an adequate job. They recognize the need for early childhood education and are helpful in getting community support for necessary programs.

Parents working in our classrooms assist in many ways. They learn to apply our procedures in their homes in order to insure continuity in their child's program; they learn to take data both in the school and at home; they encourage other parents to work effectively with their own children; they talk with their neighbors and help to dispel misconceptions about handicapped children. In short, they are supporting the staff and extending the efforts to reach and serve families of handicapped children.

Additionally, the parents respond to the many requests that come to us from other parents, reporters and site visitors for interviews; they participate in site visits; they write articles that may be helpful to other parents; and they participate in panel discussions in university classes and programs, and in workshops. They share our concerns about funding and about extending needed services to greater numbers of handicapped children. If site visitors from funding agencies want to talk with parents, we ask for volunteers from the parents. At the scheduled time—that which is most convenient for the parents—we simply introduce the parents to the site visitors and leave the room, confident that the parents know the program's goals as well as we do. Sometimes the parents sense that we have important visitors, and they seek to help even if they have not been asked to do so.

Parents have also been instrumental in establishing programs, particularly infant learning programs, in communities where none had previously existed. They continue to request assistance from our staff when it is needed, and to arrange for some of us to meet with the parents and other members of the communities in which these programs are established. They also work with school districts in urging them to extend programs, and are constantly attempting to reach parents of handicapped children in order to help them learn about the resources that are available to them and their children. They work with established agencies, organizations, and programs in their efforts to disseminate information about what can and should be done on behalf of handicapped children.

Finally, parents have been active in the movement to change legislation so that insurance companies include in their coverage provisions for children with birth defects. In light of the fact that medical and professional treatment can be extremely expensive, parents should have help in defraying such costs. Further, publicity given to such efforts to change legislation helps to alert prospective parents of the need to consider "things that could happen in any family" and to learn more about handicapping conditions that may be evident at birth.

Concluding Statement

In their efforts to provide training and assistance in meeting the needs of parents and families, professionals can learn a great deal from the parents and families themselves. That has certainly been our experience here at the Center, where we see our work with handicapped children as a working partnership with the children's parents and families.

As parents and families from the Center move out into communities and seek to establish new programs for other handicapped children and their families—programs that are badly needed but that are not now provided by any agencies—we applaud their efforts to extend services and feel a deep commitment to help them in this work. This approach may not be an ideal one—that is, some standards that the parents and we would like to set for programs cannot possibly be met initially, and it will take time and a great deal of assistance to arrive at "ideal arrangements." But these are beginning efforts and they are extremely important, for without these programs, many children and families needing special services would be denied them. There can hardly be a more appropriate "testimonial" to the parents' involvement and partnership than their determination to extend services that they have benefited from to other families. Their interest and their many forms of support are richly rewarding to us all.

Bibliography

Allen, K. "Individualizing Instruction for Preschool Children through Utilization of Parent-Teacher Data." In A.H. Hayden (Ed.), *Selected Case Studies*. Seattle: University of Washington, 1972.

Johnson, C., & Katz, R. "Using Parents as Change Agents for Their Children: A Review." *Journal of Child Psychology and Psychiatry*, 1973, 14, 181 –200.

Martz, H. "We had hoped." *United Methodist Today*, January 1974, 34–37.

Mills, D. "Things Are Looking Up For Down's Syndrome Children." *The Seattle Times Magazine*, January 6, 1974, 8–10.

A Home-Center Based Parent Training Mode

H.D. Fredricks
Victor L. Baldwin
David Grove

Most parent-training models are designed to provide training to parents whose children are not enrolled in a program. In fact, many educators take the position that if the handicapped child is enrolled in a school-type program there is little need for the parents to be trained in the techniques of teaching their own child. Two factors militate against this position. First, there is a body of evidence that indicates that if parents of children enrolled in a school or center engage in some teaching of that child, the child's learning will be significantly accelerated. This will be discussed at length later in the chapter. Second, pressure from the parents who want to participate in the teaching of their child often requires that they be taught how to teach their child.

Let us speak to the latter point first. Our experience is that many parents, especially parents of severely handicapped children,

H. D. FREDERICKS is Associate Director of Teaching Research in Monmouth, Oregon. He is especially interested in retarded, deaf, and blind children, and in the emotionally disturbed.

VICTOR L. BALDWIN is Director of the Exceptional Child Research Program at Teaching Research in Monmouth, Oregon. His areas of interest include behavior modification, measurement and evaluation, paraprofessional training, and classroom management.

DAVID N. GROVE is an Associate Research Professor at the University of Oregon in Monmouth. His specialties include physical therapy techniques, parent training, and treatment strategies.

are interested in doing as much as they can for their child and consequently are willing to undertake home programs. Moreover, as the child's success in the center program increases, parents become more eager to help their child. Frequently, they have been discouraged about their child's capabilities until the center demonstrates some success with him, at which time the parents' discouragement is replaced by optimism and a desire to contribute to their child's newfound growth. Therefore as educators we need to be responsive to these desires of the parents and instruct them in teaching their own child.

But even if the parents did not request us to provide this type of instruction, it is logical that we should involve the parents in at least some educational activities and training. For instance, it is practically impossible to toilet train a child with only a school-training program; a coordinated program between school and home is mandatory if the child is going to be completely trained before he is a teenager.

Perhaps even more critical than the child's acquisition of self-help skills is the acquisition of language skills, which also is accelerated by a home-center coordinated program. Language skills—the acquisition of sounds, blends, words, the chaining of words—can all be learned through structured programs, but it is only with the use of language in the everyday environment of the child that the handicapped child can use language fluently. Since the parents usually constitute a large portion of the child's environment and provide him with much of the feedback he receives each day, it is necessary for the parents to be actively engaged in the handicapped child's language acquisition to maximize the rate of that acquisition.

Certainly for the child to progress through the entire range of self-help skills, the parent must become involved in instructing the child. For example, if a teacher is teaching a child to take off his coat, and the child is required to do as much of that behavior as he is able to at school, it is defeating for the parents to assist the child in taking off his coat at home to a degree greater than assistance is given at school. Development of each of the self-help skills—dressing, self-feeding, personal hygiene—benefits from a very closely coordinated program with the parents.

It is our experience that not only in the areas mentioned above can parents be good teachers, but that they can be effective in any area of instruction. This effectiveness is demonstrated by the acceleration in the rate with which children learn and the quality and quantity of what they learn. In brief, if a parent will conduct for ten

minutes to a half hour a day a training program at home in conjunction with the same training program being conducted at the school,
the child will acquire the taught skill in a significantly quicker time.
In fact the datas show that the systematic program involving the
parent in conjunction with the school program will almost double
the rate of acquisition of the skill. (For a more complete discussion
of this acceleration rate see the evaluation section of this chapter.)

This chapter will describe three variations of the home-center
model which have been used with children who have various handicaps, including deafness and blindness, mental retardation, emotional disturbances and learning disabilities. Thus the model has
universal applicability across all handicapping conditions. The
three variations of the home-center model are: (1) The Lunch Box
Data System, in which parents conduct instruction at home similar
to that being conducted at the school; (2) The Modified Lunch Box
System, in which parents conduct instruction at home that is not
being given by the school; and (3) the Volunteer System, in which
parents are volunteer workers at the school and through that experience acquire the instructional capabilities to teach their own child.

The Lunch Box Data System

Intake.   In the home-center model, the children are already students in the center and so we shall not discuss how these children
are taken into the program. We shall, however, focus on how we
take parents into this program.

We think that the parents of every child who is in the program
should be given the opportunity to conduct at least one home-
training program. To start this process a group meeting is held with
the parents. They can all be brought together in a large group, or
invited to participate in smaller groups according to their child's
classroom, age, or handicapping condition. The purpose of the
meeting is to explain home-training programs and "sell" the idea of
participating in a program to the parents. Two major "selling"
points have been found to be successful. First, the accelerated rate
at which the child can acquire skills should be demonstrated to the
parents by specific examples. Second, the necessity for the generalization from center to home of the child's learning, especially in the
areas of self-help skills, toilet training and language acquisition,
should be stressed.

After this group meeting, individual conferences are scheduled
with the parents to determine which program the parent desires to

Figure 12

Task Analysis of the Dressing Skill
of
Removing Pants, Underpants

Steps

1. Child grabs cuffs and removes pants when one leg removed.
2. Child grabs cuffs and removes pants when pulled to ankles.
3. Child pushes down to ankles, grabs cuffs and removes pants when pulled to knees.
4. Child pushes down to ankles, grabs cuffs and removes pants when pulled to thighs.
5. Child pushes down to ankles, grabs cuffs and removes pants.

conduct at home. Parents should be encouraged to conduct language acquisition and self-help skill programs if the child is participating in such programs in the center, but they may initially choose a motor program or one in a cognitive area, such as reading or arithmetic. If at all possible the parents' choice should be honored because this choice probably represents their priority of what their child should be taught. It probably also represents skills, which, if the child acquires, will be reinforcing to the parent.

Great care must be exercised in this initial selection of a program. One of the primary considerations in this selection is to choose a program with the parent that is likely to succeed: such as simple self-help skills like dressing, cognitive skills like rote counting, sound recognition, shape sorting; and certain motor tasks. It should almost go without saying that we would not pick as an initial skill to be taught one which we have been teaching in the center but with which progress has been slow.

Regardless of which skill we choose, we must further the likelihood of success by breaking this skill into small parts (task analysis) and showing the parents how to teach one part at a time. Figure 12 shows the task analysis for the behavior of removing underpants. If the parents are faced with having to teach only one small step at a time rather than the entire task, the chances for the parents to see some progress are greater, and thus the parents will be reinforced for their efforts. Once the program has been selected, the parent is ready to be trained.

Direct Services Delivery. It should be pointed out here that the effectiveness of any parental involvement program is largely dependent on how precise the instructions are that are given to the parents. General instructions will only confuse and frustrate the parents and make them feel guilty when they are not successful. The more specific the program, the less chance there is for failure.

After the program has been selected by the parent and the teacher, the teacher models the program for the parent. During the course of this modeling the teacher demonstrates to the parents all aspects of the teaching paradigm. First, the teacher demonstrates the physical position of the child in relationship to the teacher and the preparation and placement of any cues that may be necessary or materials that may be needed. For instance, when a teacher is demonstrating how to teach a deaf and blind child to take off his socks, the positioning of the teacher and the child is extremely important. The child should be placed in a position sitting on the floor with the teacher behind him, with her legs straddling the child so that she can reach easily over his shoulders if necessary and guide his hands to the socks and through the motions. Likewise, if the teacher is teaching a word recognition program to a child and using picture cards to elicit the words, the placement and the method of presentation of the cards must be stressed and modeled for the parents.

Once the preparation of cues and the placement of the child have been modeled, the teacher must demonstrate precisely the way in which cues are to be given. Imagine a child who is on a program to increase the number of seconds the child attends to the teacher's voice. The preciseness with which the child is told to attend is important. For instance, the cue might be, "Look, Johnny," and if the child were deaf a sign might also be emitted by the teacher. The teacher may also desire to touch the child to get his attention initially. All of these fine points of the presentation of the cue must be adequately explained and modeled for the parents by the teacher.

The precision with which cues are given of course is in direct relationship to the severity of the handicap of the child. The more severe the handicap, the more precise must be the cue. The less severe the handicap, the less precision is required in the delivery of the cue, although a certain amount of consistency on the part of the parent should be stressed.

The expected behavior that the child is to emit after the delivery of the cue should be explained to the parent. Any shaping procedures that are being utilized or the degree of precision with which the child must emit should all be included in the instruction.

For instance a child is being taught to write the capital letter A. What degree of precision must be expected? Is this correct? A̱ Is this correct? *A* or is this correct? *A* Hopefully the teacher has pre-scribed what degree of acceptability marks success and what is not considered correct. The parent must be willing to accept the teacher's criteria for success. This acceptance will be facilitated by explaining the shaping process—how we first accept a capital A that looks like this: *A*. Then we shall demand that the point of the A start on the line so we then shall accept anything resembling an A as long as the apex is on the line, such as *A*. Then, we may require the base of the left leg of the A to stop on the bottom line, and so on until we have step-by-step shaped the child's letter-writing ability.

During the modeling stage the teacher demonstrates the way in which to deliver the consequences to the child for the behavior emitted. If the behavior is correct, the teacher demonstrates the way in which to deliver reinforcers, both social and tangible, paying particular attention to the pairing of tangible and social conse-quences. If signing is required, the delivery of the sign, the verbali-zation and the delivery of the tangible consequence in rapid succes-sion is a difficult thing to coordinate and must be demonstrated precisely in a set order to the parent.

The method of delivering the negative feedback, or the "No, that is not right, Johnny," when the child makes an incorrect re-sponse as well as how to perform a correction procedure, should be demonstrated to the parent. Again, the accuracy of this correction procedure and the speed and precision of the delivery of the conse-quences are important to the child. The more severely handicapped the child is, the greater necessity there is to deliver reinforcers or negative feedback promptly. The more severely handicapped the child, the more precise the correction procedure must be when the child emits an incorrect response. In order to emphasize the instruc-tions we give to parents of more severely handicapped children, we have the parents read selected portions of *Isn't It Time He Outgrew This?* by Victor L. Baldwin, H. D. Bud Fredericks and Gerry Brodsky (Charles C. Thomas, 1973). All parents are asked to read the initial chapters on cues, behaviors, consequences and data keep-ing. Additional chapters are read to coordinate with the behavior being taught. For instance, the chapter on dressing would be read if the parents were teaching their child to dress or undress. In addition, there are chapters discussing self-feeding, toilet training, hygiene habits, language acquisition, motor skills, and academic learning.

Once the teacher has modeled the entire procedure a number of times to the parent, the parent is asked to try the procedure with her child in the presence of the teacher. At this point in time, if videotape cameras are available, they can be used to film the parent's attempts and thus facilitate the instructional process. Then, in addition to the feedback given to the parent by the teacher as the program is conducted with the child, the parent can watch a playback of the videotape and more vividly understand the corrections which the teacher has been giving to her. In correcting the parent during the videotape playback, however, emphasis should be placed on the positive aspects of the parents' performance. Too frequently we focus only on the poor aspects.

Once the parent has demonstrated that he or she can deliver the cues and consequences to the child correctly and does so three or four times in a row, the parent is then informed of the extent of the program and the subsequent sequences of the program. For instance Figure 12 shows a sequence for a dressing skill—removing underpants. If the child is on step one, the parent is instructed to work on that step until the child makes three correct responses in a row. Then the parent is to move automatically to step two. Perhaps a demonstration of the entire sequence might be necessary at this time.

Since the same program is being conducted in the home as in the center it is important that this program be coordinated between the two environments. Therefore, a data system must be developed for passing information about the child's progress back and forth between the parent and the center on a daily basis. We have dubbed this daily reporting system the Lunch Box Data System. Figure 13 is a data sheet for the dressing program shown in Figure 12 that is passed back and forth between center and home. The instructions to the parents before these data were taken were to move to the next step of the program if the child was able to do a step three times in a row successfully. Figure 13 shows the data as submitted by the parent after fifteen minutes of trying the program at home one evening. The child obviously was able to do step one after a few minutes and then did step two successfully two times. Therefore, the teacher in the classroom the next day, on receiving these data, will work with the child on step two. Let us suppose for the sake of the example that the teacher achieves success with step two. She then sends home the data sheet to the parent marked as shown in Figure 14, which indicates to the parent that she is to work with the child on step three. This type of daily communication is imperative if the teacher and the parent are to coordinate their instructional activity with the child so that there is no lost time in the teaching of this child.

Figure 13

Data for Dressing Program
Being Coordinated at Home

Child's Name _Johnnie_   STEPS

1. _____ 6. _____
2. _____ 7. _____
3. _____ 8. _____
4. _____ 9. _____
5. _____ 10. _____

Date	Reinforcer Used	Phase	Step	Trials										Comments
				1	2	3	4	5	6	7	8	9	10	
2/4/76	Juice-social	II	1	X	O	X	O	X	X	X				
2/4/76	Juice-social		2	O	X	X								

home

Figures 15, 16, 17, and 18 show two ways in which teachers in two different types of programs provide information for parents about the program which they are conducting. Such directions have been found to facilitate the communication process between the center and the home. Although the teacher has spent additional time modeling, demonstrating and explaining the program to the parents at the center, the parents may have some questions when they try the program at home without assistance. These written directions help to answer some of those questions. The amount of detail put into these types of communication varies considerably from teacher to teacher and center to center. Figure 15 shows a home program for a child in the Medford preschool which caters primarily to children with learning disabilities and educable mentally retarded children, and Figures 16, 17 and 18 show the program sheet that will be sent home together with a sequence for a child in the Teaching Research Multiple Handicap Preschool.

Liaison and Follow-Through. The parent will continue to run the program, and data will continue to circulate back and forth between the school and the home. Frequently the parent may experience problems. The parent should communicate these as rapidly as possible to the teacher so that the teacher can take remedial action. Often when the parent has such problems, the parent should be brought into the school to observe teachers modeling and to demonstrate how she is conducting the program at home in order to isolate the problem.

Even if the parent is not experiencing problems with the program, periodic conferences—at least every three to four weeks—are recommended. During these conferences the parent should once again demonstrate how she is conducting the program at home. All teachers sometimes acquire some bad habits, and parents are not exempt from this fault. Thus, this periodic conference serves as a maintenance check on the quality of the home program.

One of the center activities that the parents seem to enjoy is periodic parent meetings. During the meetings they share the experiences that they have been having in teaching children. This type of conference is especially valuable for those parents who may be having some difficulties; after listening to how other parents are solving problems, they may be encouraged to try even harder. For parents who are having success, the opportunity to voice that success publicly can be very reinforcing and may help to insure their continuance in the program.

Evaluation

Evaluation of this kind of program can be done on at least two dimensions. The first is program-wide. What percentage of the parents are participating in this type of program? Our experience indicates that the average center will have about 50 percent of their parents actively running home programs. Of this 50 percent about one-fourth will require rather close monitoring and frequent liaison on the part of the teacher. The teacher should not become discouraged if certain parents refuse to participate in this program or if certain parents who initially agree to participate drop out. It would be an extraordinary program which had more than 60 percent of the parents participating on a continuing basis in this type of home program. The teacher should strive to prescribe some modeling and instruction to all parents and have the parents demonstrate how they would provide the instruction. Much of this procedure learned by the parent can be used even though it may not be on a consistent, daily basis.

Another way to look at program evaluation is the number of programs which each parent conducts. All participating parents should be conducting at least one program nightly, although it is not unusual to find some parents who will conduct three or four nightly.

A final dimension upon which the value of this kind of home-center program can be judged is the progress of the children. Figures 19 and 20 show graphs of children's progress in this type of program. Figure 19 shows a Downs Syndrome child who was first taught to read sight words in the center only. This method of teaching was followed by a coordinated home and center program. The data demonstrate that after the home and center program was initiated the child's progress accelerated rapidly. Figure 20 shows a graph of a child who is learning to rote count in a learning disability preschool; the data indicate that after the parents became involved in conducting home programs and helping the child to learn to rote count, the acceleration of his skills was quite rapid. Although these kinds of data have been replicated frequently in this type of home-center program, the evaluation which each center must undertake of this type of program must be on an individual basis, monitoring each child's progress very carefully. The Lunch Box Data System allows that kind of monitoring and evaluating.

Figure 14

Data for Dressing Program
Being Coordinated at Home and School

Child's Name *Johnnie*

Steps

1. ______ 6. ______
2. ______ 7. ______
3. ______ 8. ______
4. ______ 9. ______
5. ______ 10. ______

	Date	Reinforcer Used	Phase	Step	Trials 1	2	3	4	5	6	7	8	9	10	Comments
home	*2/4/76*	*juice-social*	*II*	*1*	X	O	X	O	X	X	X				
school	*2/4/76*	*juice-social.*		*2*	O	X	X								
	2/5/76	*juice-social*		*2*	O	X	O	X	X	X					
	2/5/76			*3*											

Figure 15

Home Program for
Medford Preschool

ROUTE COUNTING

Child __Mike__   Date Initiated __11/3/75__   Teacher __Mrs. Barnard__

Goal:

__Mike__ will be able to count by himself to __40__ without error four days in a row.

Procedure:

Help your child feel good about himself. Praise him whenever possible. Try to work with your child at the same time every day.

1. Count to __40__ with __Mike__.

2. Using the cup and _____ beans, have __Mike__ count each bean as he drops it in a cup.

3. __Mike__ counts to __13__ by himself.

Each day record the number your child can count to by himself.

Reward:

This should be a realistic and practical choice. __go to Mac Donalds__

Suggested period of time for working with child each day: __5-10 minutes__

Schedule for evaluation

Date to be returned		
	Yes	No
11/5	✓	
11/6	✓	

Date to be returned		
	Yes	No
11/17		
11/18		

Date to be returned		
	Yes	No
11/19		

Figure 16

Home Program for Teaching Research
Multiple Handicap Preschool

Name: _Susie_____ Date started: _1/25/75_ Date completed: _____

Task objective: _Child will imitate 2-3-4 word chains._____

Materials and Setting: _objects and/or pictures of the words you're working on._

Treatment:

　1. Cue or instructions:

　　A. Verbal: _"Look, Susie, say_____."_____

　　B. Non-verbal: _Present picture or object as you say the phrase._

　　C. Incorrect response: _"No, Susie."_____

Criterion level of acceptable behavior: _5 consecutive correct responses_
before going on to next word chain.

Modified Lunch Box System

In the modified Lunch Box System the home-center model as pre-viously described is followed except that the parent conducts pro-grams with the child that are not conducted at the school. Another term for this model might be the supplementary or modified Lunch Box Model.

Intake.   Again children are already in the center receiving in-struction. This model is usually initiated when the parent ap-proaches the teacher and states that she would like to work on a program at home which is not being conducted in the center. This request should immediately cause the center to examine the pro-grams which they are conducting with the child, for if the parent is placing such a high priority on this additional program, perhaps the program should be conducted in the center. However, often this is not possible; the problem is manifested only at home.

Delivery of Direct Services.   In the Lunch Box Model, the collec-tion of baseline data is part of the routine data-gathering system within the center. However, in the Modified Lunch Box Model, no baseline data have been gathered in the center and therefore the first step in this modified approach must be to gather such data. If the information to be gathered has to do with the acquisition of a skill, it should be easily collected at the center. If an inappropriate behavior is being manifested in the home, baseline data will have to be gathered there. The parent then will have to be instructed how to do this. For instance, let us suppose that the child is exhib-iting temper tantrums in the home but not in the school. For base-line data the teacher may request that the parent count the number of temper tantrums and the length of each temper tantrum over a three-day period.

Once the necessary baseline data have been gathered, the proce-dure for conducting and monitoring the program is essentially the same as the Lunch Box System, except that since the program is not being carried out in the school as well as at home, it is not neces-sary for the teacher to monitor the data daily, although the parents may request that the teacher do so. Data submitted every three to five days by the parent should be sufficient for the teacher to modify the program as necessary to insure that the child is making progress.

It should be recognized that if this modified program requires the parent to teach the child a skill, the teacher should demonstrate it for the parent and carry out the entire modeling procedure described in the Lunch Box Model. Furthermore, the teacher's written instructions for the parent should be very specific and precise. If the parent decides to deviate in any way from those instructions, the parent should be asked to consult the teacher.

Liaison and Follow-Through. Periodic liaison is maintained with the parent on a three-to-five day basis and the programs are modified based on the data at that time. Certainly if the parent is having difficulty she should feel free to call the teacher and arrange for a conference so as to make early modification in the program.

Evaluation. On a program-wide scale the number of these types of programs should be tracked and examined to determine that there are no deficits in the center programming for the children which necessitate these additional programs in the home. On an individual child basis, however, the data should indicate the progress of the child and how well the program is working.

One case study of a child on a modified Lunch Box System follows. It illustrates how a center should keep individualized data. Figure 21 shows data for a family whose child is in the Teaching Research Infant and Child Center multiple handicapped classroom. The parents were having difficulty with the child's responding to commands or instructions. In fact, the child's compliance rate was so low that the parent suspected that the child might have a hearing defect. Yet, the Center was not experiencing a similar difficulty. When the child first entered the Center, the first few days were spent bringing some inappropriate behaviors under control, but there was no continual difficulty with compliance.

Consultation was held with the parent about the difficulty she was experiencing at home. Baseline data indicated that the child was complying 40 percent of the time.

A program was initiated in which the parent was required to exaggerate the consequences for the child's compliance and for non-compliance. At the time of this writing, the program is continuing but the compliance rate at home has reached 82 percent, and the parent is in the process of fading the primary reinforcers used in the program.

The Parent as a Volunteer

Intake. Oftentimes parents are willing to serve as volunteers in the child center. Every opportunity should be made to utilize these parents in the actual instruction of children because as they

Figure 17

Child's Name _____

Criterion: _5 consecutive correct_

responses

1 = Correct response
0 = Incorrect response

Behavior	Baseline	Date				
Phases:	ll 1/25	1/28	1/29	1/30	2/3	2/4
1. a boy	/	⑦⑦⑦/				
2. a girl	/	⑦⑦⑦/				
3. a shirt		⑦⑦⑦//				
4. the dress	/	⑦⑦⑦				
5. the milk	/	⑦⑦⑦				
6. the cake	/		111011			
7. a bed	/		⑦⑦⑦			
8. a chair	/		⑦⑦⑦			
9. red ball	/		⑦⑦⑦			
10. a car	/		⑦⑦⑦			
11. the dog	/ s/d			000⑦⑦⑦		
12. the cat	/			⑦⑦⑦		
13. a house	/			⑦⑦⑦		
14. a boat	/			⑦⑦⑦		
15. a baby	/				⑦⑦⑦	
16. the candy	/				⑦⑦⑦	
17. red wagon	0				111010	⑦⑦⑦
Teaching Time	5 min.	15 min.	15 min.	15 min.	tired tonight 15 min.	

Figure 18

Child's Name _____

Criterion: _5 consecutive_

correct responses.

1 = Correct response
0 = Incorrect response

Behavior	Date				
	2/3	2/4			
a toothbrush	001	(HHH)			
Susie is eating	(HHH)				
Susie is washing		100(HHH)			
Susie is writing		110101			
Susie is dancing					
Susie is running					
Susie is sleeping					
Susie is ironing					
Teaching Time	15 min.	15 min.			

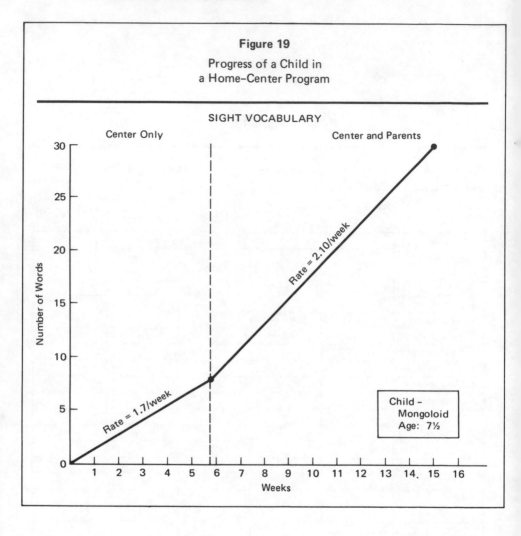

Figure 19

Progress of a Child in
a Home–Center Program

learn how to instruct children in the center, they will be able to instruct and guide their own child in the home more effectively. It is a rare parent who works in an effective child center who has not learned to present cues and consequences properly, who has not learned to analyze a task, and who has not seen the necessity for the maintenance of data to insure more efficient programming of children.

A group meeting of parents might be held to obtain volunteers. The topic of parents' volunteering should be presented and explained. The presentation of videotapes of parents at work in the center is particularly effective. Emphasis on the benefits that will accrue to their own child may "sell" some parents on the idea.

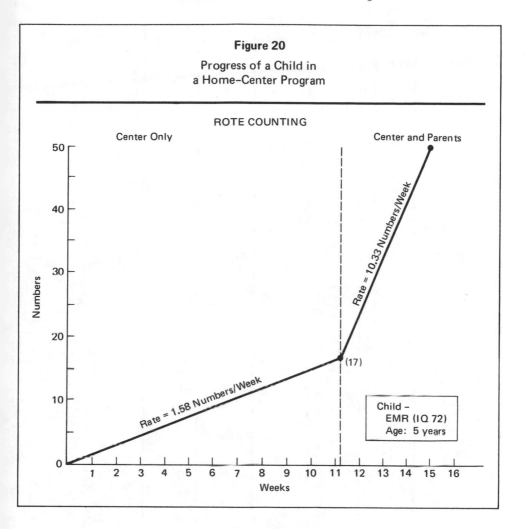

Figure 20

Progress of a Child in
a Home–Center Program

ROTE COUNTING

Center Only

Center and Parents

Rate = 1.58 Numbers/Week

Rate = 10.33 Numbers/Week

(17)

Child –
EMR (IQ 72)
Age: 5 years

Numbers

Weeks

Service Delivery.   Once the parents have agreed to volunteer, they must go through a training period. The limits of this chapter do not allow a complete discussion of the training that should be conducted for a parent volunteer. However, we have found certain rules for training to be effective guidelines. In short, some of these guidelines are:

- Time must be taken to train volunteers and the training must be concise and simple. A short lecture describing the center, the things a volunteer must do, and some principles of teaching is an excellent way to begin. This lecture is followed by

Figure 21

Home Program for Inappropriate Behavior
Teaching Research Infant and Child Center

Name _____ *Tim* _____ Date started _____ *December 13, 1975* _____

Date completed/terminated _____

Task Objective:

Increase command compliance to 85%, between 9:00 AM and 1:00 PM for seven consecutive days. The 85% will be an average for the seven day period.

Baseline Data:

12/14	50%	12/16	33%	12/8	25%	$\bar{X} = 40\%$
12/15	33%	12/17	50%	12/19	40%	

Final Data:

If program not completed but terminated, state reason:

Treatment:

	START DATE	FINISH DATE
1. *Reinforce w/ food for each compliance.*	12/20/75	
2. *Reinforce w/ food for each compliance. Punish w/ firm verbal "no" for each non-compliance.*	1/03/76	
3. *Reinforce w/ food for each compliance. Punish w/ 3 minute time-out.*	1/10/76	

Figure 21 (Continued)

Child's Name _____ Tim _____

Program
Initiated _____ December 14, 1975 _____

Terminated _____

Percentage of Correct Responses

Baseline   sR+ = food   sR+ = food   sR+ = food

sR− = verbal "no"   sR− = time-out

Sessions

observation and demonstration, and, finally, the volunteer should be placed in a practicum situation in which he teaches children under supervision of a teacher or an aide.

- Volunteers must be given teaching tasks in the classroom comparable to their level of training. It will take time for parents to learn how to teach all parts of the curriculum. Starting them in one area—such as self-help, motor, development, or arithmetic—will allow them to master that area before they are required to teach in another.

- A continuous system of feedback as to the adequacy of the volunteers' performance must exist. The center must have a system of observing volunteers that allows center supervisory personnel to monitor the quality of the volunteer's teaching and to give feedback to volunteers.

- A simplified system of communication between the teacher and the volunteer that does not require oral instruction must exist. The teacher should write down specified, detailed directions on how instruction is to be delivered to children. The volunteer must record the performance of the child in some systematic way, and the recorded data must be examined on a regular basis by the teacher in order to provide timely updating of children's programs.

- A system of flexible scheduling of volunteers must be maintained. The center must be prepared for volunteers to miss days. The scheduling must allow for that possibility. It must also accommodate the training level of the volunteer.

For a more complete discussion of the guidelines, see *A Data Based Preschool for the Multiple Handicapped* by H. D. Bud Fredericks, Victor L. Baldwin, David Grove, William Moore, Charles C. Thomas (in press).

Liaison and Follow-Through. Ideally, once the parents have learned these skills of teaching in the center, it would seem that they should also be able to take those skills and utilize them in the home with their own child. If such a parent is not already conducting home programs, every effort should be made to encourage her to do so. She is then ready to move into the Lunch Box Data system.

Evaluation. Evaluation of parents' participation as volunteers can be done on two dimensions. First, program-wise, a simple count of how many parents volunteer is useful. Certainly we would expect at least 25 percent of the nonworking mothers to volunteer at least one day a week in the center.

The other dimension upon which the effectiveness of parents as volunteers can be measured is their success as teachers, which can be measured by tabulating their efficiency in dispensing cues and consequences, and the way in which they keep data and help manage the children.

Bibliography

Baldwin, V. L., Fredericks, H. D., & Brodsky, G. *Isn't It Time He Outgrew This?* or "A Training Program for Parents of Retarded Children." Springfield, Illinois: Charles C. Thomas, 1973.

Fredericks, H. D., Baldwin, V. L., Grove, D., & Moore, W. *A Data-Based Preschool for the Multiple Handicapped.* Springfield, Illinois: Charles C. Thomas, 1975.

A Home-Based Parent-Training Model

Marsha S. Shearer

The basic operational premises of the Portage Project, as they relate to parents, are: (1) parents care about their children and want them to attain their maximum potential, however great or limited that potential may be; (2) parents can, with instruction, modeling, and reinforcement, learn to be more effective teachers of their own children; (3) the socio-economic and educational or intellectual levels of the parents do not determine either their willingness to teach their children or the extent of gains the children will attain as a result of parental instruction; (4) the precision-teaching method is the preferred learning model, since feedback is provided daily to parents and weekly to staff, thereby reinforcing both when goals are met. Moreover, the method provides a continual data base for curriculum modification, thus maximizing the likelihood of success for parents and children.

Overview and Rationale of the Home-Based Program

The Portage Project operates administratively through a regional educational agency serving twenty-three districts in south-central rural Wisconsin. The project presently serves 160 children, birth to school age, who have been identified as being handicapped in one or more developmental areas. Any preschool child, with any type or

MARSHA S. SHEARER is Training Coordinator for the Portage Project in Portage, Wisconsin. Her specialties include: training parents, parent involvement programs, and precision teaching techniques.

severity of handicap residing within the 3,600-square-mile area served by the agency, qualifies for the early intervention project.

In the Portage Project there is no classroom program. Instead of having children come into a center, we use "home teachers" to visit in every child's home, where they instruct the child's parents in how to teach their own child. So our model is completely home-based, rather than center-based, and parents with the help of home teachers do all the teaching of their own children.

Three practical factors influenced our decision to have an exclusively home-based program. The first was that we were dealing with such a large geographical area that the cost and responsibility of transporting very young handicapped children great distances was prohibitive. Second, even when several children were identified within a smaller geographical area, such as one school district, the variance in chronological ages, functioning levels, and handicapping conditions precluded the possibility of establishing classroom programs. Finally, classroom programs would have severely limited parent involvement because of the geographical and psychological distances between home and school. On the basis of these factors we decided that all instruction would take place in the parent and child's natural environment—the home.

To implement this program, a home teacher is assigned to each child and family. This educator, who may be a trained professional or a trained paraprofessional, visits each of the assigned fifteen families one day per week for one and a half hours. An individual curriculum is prescribed weekly, based on an assessment of each child's present behavior in the areas of language, self-help, cognitive, motor, and social skills. Utilizing the parents as teachers, the Portage Project follows the precision teaching model which is comprised of these elements: (1) at least three behavioral goals are selected for the child to learn each week. The goals and criteria for accomplishing them are chosen so that the child, and thus the parent, will achieve success within a one week period of time; (2) baseline data is recorded by the home teacher on each new task prior to instruction as an additional check on the readiness of the child to proceed with the learning activities; (3) the parents implement the actual teaching process itself, including reinforcement of desired behavior and reduction or extinction of behavior that interferes with learning appropriate skills; and (4) the home teacher records post-baseline data one week after the baseline is taken to determine if the prescribed skills have, in fact, been learned.

The purpose of the weekly home visit is to instruct the parents in what to teach, how to teach, what to reinforce, and how to observe and record behavior. The home teacher instructs the parents (or siblings or parent substitute) during the home visit. Then, the parents or substitute teach the child and record his progress daily throughout the following week.

In this model there are certain practical advantages—not having to transport children or provide a center facility—that reduce the cost of the program by more than half. But even more importantly, there are inherent advantages that the Portage Project staff has experienced in the home-based, precision teaching model. These advantages are based on involving the child's first, and potentially his best, teachers—his parents. The educational assets that we found are:

- The parent teaches the child in his natural environment. Therefore, they do not have the problem of transferring learning into the home as they would if the child were in a center-based program.
- This model is totally dependent on parent involvement for success. Since one and a half hours one day per week is not a sufficient amount of time for a child to learn developmental skills from the home teacher, parents must be taught to teach their own child between home visits. Thus, training parents is more than a program adjunct—it is absolutely mandatory.
- Another major advantage in using the home-based precision teaching model is that the home teacher and the parents have direct access to the child's behavior as it occurs naturally. This situation engenders realistic curriculum goals that will be functional for the child within his unique environment. In fact, the differences in cultures, life styles, and value systems of parents are incorporated into curriculum planning, since the parents determine what and how their child will be taught.
- It is more likely that the skills that the child learns will generalize to other areas and be maintained if the skills have been learned in the child's home environment and taught by the child's natural reinforcing agent—his parents.
- Father, sibling, and extended family involvement become a realistic and obtainable goal. When instruction occurs in the home there is more opportunity for full family participation in the teaching process.
- There is access to the full range of the child's behavior: such as temper tantrums, which only occur in the home, or hearing from the parents that their child is crawling into bed

with them each night. Much of this behavior could not be targeted for modification within a classroom.

- Finally, since the home teacher is working on a one-to-one basis with the parents and child, individualization of instructional goals for both is a reality rather than an idealized goal.

Parent Participation in the Intake and Assessment Process

After a child has been referred to the Project (parents can and often do refer their own children), a home teacher contacts the parents and makes an appointment to visit the home to explain the project and meet and screen the child.

It is at this time that parents are told that they will teach their own child and that they will learn how to teach him by observing the instruction given by the home teacher. The following are examples of a few typical reactions of parents and resultant responses of the home teachers at this point.

- Parent: "Oh, I've tried teaching Mary, like how to walk, but she can't even crawl yet."
  Teacher: "Maybe teaching Mary how to crawl, if she's ready, would be a good place for us to begin."
- Parent: "We're not trained teachers; we can't do anything as important as that."
  Teacher: "You've been teaching Jim all along. Just look at all the things he can do. He makes sounds, he's beginning to feed himself, he matches objects, he points to body parts. You've taught him a lot!"
- Parents: "We've given up trying to accomplish anything. He just drives us crazy. You teach him and leave us out of it."
  Teacher: "I can't. I need you and so does Chris. While I'm here, I'll show you what to do and how to do it. I'm not going to ask you to try anything without showing you first that it's going to work. So let's give it a try together."
- Parent: "Oh, I don't have time to teach Todd."
  Teacher: "You do spend some time with Todd each day don't you? Okay, all I'm asking is that you spend that time working on these activities. I promise they won't take more than a half hour a day. And yell any time if you think it's too much."
- Parent: "I have no patience. I don't think I can do it."
  Teacher: "Sure you can, I'll give you all the help you need.

Give the program a try for a month or so. If you don't think we're getting anywhere, you're free to withdraw at any time. But give it a try first."

- Parent: I work all day, don't get home 'till 6:00 and by then I'm exhausted. I fix dinner for Dawn, then she goes to bed. There's just no time for me to work with her."

  Teacher: "I'll be happy to work with Dawn's babysitter, and I'll call you each week to keep you posted so you'll know how she's doing and what to work on during the weekend."

But the most frequent reaction to our approach to parents is, "We've never gotten any practical help 'till now. Every time I take her in for an evaluation, we're told nothing. Oh, they tell us Penny will never walk and that she might be blind. But no one has ever told us what we can do to help."

After six years of working with nearly 500 parents, we have found that the most frequent question asked during the initial visit is, "What can I do with my child; how can I help him learn?" Parents are accustomed to hearing what their child isn't doing, so it isn't surprising that they stress the negative too. And this brings us to the assessment process.

The child is screened during this first visit to determine project eligibility. All screening is done in the home with the parents' consent and help, which includes contributing their knowledge of the child. The screening instrument (Alpern and Boll, 1972) which is also used as one of the pre and post measures, is administered as a parental questionnaire together with direct observation of the child's behavior, when possible. In fact, assessment couldn't be accomplished without them. We have found that the results are likely to be more reliable than if testing were done without the benefit of parent involvement because parents know their children best. Also, since the assessment instruments are administered on the parent and child's "home ground," results are likely to be more accurate than if the assessment were attempted in a strange environment.

The assessment of the child also becomes the first step in parent training. During this process questions are asked by the home teacher concerning the child's present behavior in five different areas of growth and development. Many parents voice surprise at how much they know about their child in some areas and how little they know about their child in others. Parents make general remarks like: "I must have seen Johnny go up and down steps hundreds of times, but I just haven't noticed if he does it with two feet on the same step or if he walks down like I do." If the parent is unsure of the answer to any question, the home teacher tests the child directly.

Many parents verbalize that they don't know if their child can cut with scissors or ride a trike because they haven't given him the opportunity. Often, just asking the parents the questions gives them the clue to try. One parent called the office two days after initial assessment to report that not only could Suzie now cut paper following a straight line but she also took advantage of her new-found skill and gave the family dog a haircut! (Fortunately, the mother was laughing.)

In addition to the Alpern-Boll, the Portage Checklist is also completed (Shearer, Billingsley, Frohman, et al 1972). A description of this instrument along with descriptions of other project components can be found elsewhere (Shearer and Shearer, 1972; Frohman and Schortinghuis, in press). This instrument lists a series of behavioral sequences from birth to age five encompassing self-help, motor, language, socialization and cognitive skills. This checklist aids the parent and teacher in breaking developmental tasks into smaller steps and then assessing whether the child exhibits the behavior on entry into the program. What the child can already do determines what he's ready to learn next. The results of the assessment are discussed with the parents. All of the parents' questions regarding the assessment are answered honestly and in understandable language without psycho-educational jargon. When we discuss the assessment with the parent, we emphasize what the child can do. This is because the curriculum the parent will be asked to carry out will be based on what he is ready to learn next. The process itself sometimes makes parents aware of the accomplishments of their children. One father said, "You know, up to this point, all I've really noticed are all the things Ronnie can't do. Guess he's accomplished a few things after all."

After the assessment is completed the home teaching process begins. Based on information from the assessment, the home teacher often points out three or four behavioral goals that are emerging. The parents are given the choice as to which behavioral goal they would like to target first.

Parent Participation in the Delivery of Services—The Home-Visit Process

The home teacher writes up an activity chart incorporating the parents' selection of behavioral goals (see Figures 22 and 23). The most important point here is for the home teacher to break tasks down and prescribe only those which are most likely to be achieved within one week. When success on these tasks is achieved the parents are immediately reinforced because what was learned by the child was a direct result of parental teaching. The directions are written in simple, clear language so that the parents can effectively refer to them during the week. The parents are asked to keep simple records on the activity chart. Recording is uncomplicated and usually involves frequency counts.

First the home teacher introduces the activity to the child and records the frequency of correct responses prior to instruction. This baseline data is recorded on the activity chart. The home teacher begins the teaching process by following the written directions on the activity sheet. The home teacher is thus modeling teaching techniques for the parents—showing them what to do and how to do it. After several trials, the parents model for the home teacher. Extra activity sheets are provided so the parents can practice recording the child's behavior as they work with him while the home teacher is still there. The home teacher then is able to offer suggestions and reinforcement that will maximize the likelihood that the parents will work effectively with the child during the week and then the child will succeed with the prescribed activity.

Throughout the visit the home teacher stresses the importance of working with the child during the week. The home teacher leaves his or her home and office phone number with the parents and encourages them to call if any question or problem arises during the week. The home teacher returns the following week to collect post-baseline data on the previous week's activities. This helps the teacher validate the accuracy of the parents' recording and provides the teacher with feedback concerning the degree of success achieved by the child and his readiness to proceed to the next sequential step. Based on this data, the home teacher prepares a new activity sheet. On this new sheet the previous prescriptions are altered or new activities are introduced. Baseline data is recorded and so the cycle is repeated. At the completion of each home visit, the parent writes an evaluation of the week's progress, which often serves as an additional source of information for curriculum planning and modification.

Every attempt is made to utilize materials available in the home; however, there are times when materials are brought in and left for the parents to use. This works well because parents take care of materials. During the past five years, only 2 percent of these materials have been lost or broken.

This is the basic sequence of the home visit process. However

Figure 22
Activity Sheet

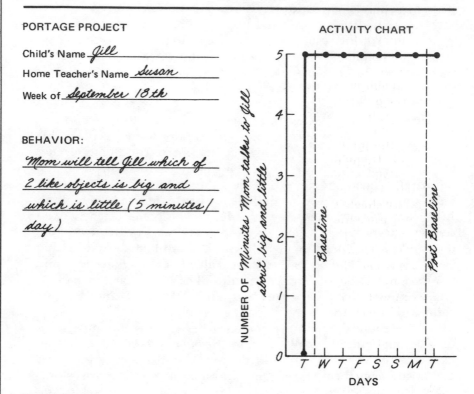

PORTAGE PROJECT

Child's Name _Jill_

Home Teacher's Name _Susan_

Week of _September 18th_

BEHAVIOR:

_Mom will tell Jill which of
2 like objects is big and
which is little (5 minutes/
day)_

ACTIVITY CHART

NUMBER OF Minutes Mom talks to Jill about big and little

Baseline

Post Baseline

DAYS

T W T F S S M T

DIRECTIONS:

1. _Use paired objects or pictures that are the same — except
   for size._

2. _Talk with Jill pointing to and naming the objects that
   are big and little, and encourage Jill to repeat the size
   word in imitation of you._

3. _Praise her each time she imitates._

4. _Use as many different examples of like pictures and
   objects as possible._

5. _Record the number of minutes you spend naming big
   and little each day._

in reality, sometimes modifications of the process are necessary. Parents are not the same, thus it is as important to individualize the teaching process for them as it is to do so with their child. The following are examples of how the process has been modified to accommodate individual differences among parents.

Parents Who Cannot Read or Write or Who Are Themselves Handicapped. One family had eight children, seven of whom were in special education classes. The youngest, a preschooler, was at home and had been referred to the Project by the county nurse. The father kept all intruders away from the house with a shotgun and greeted the home teacher in this manner; however, both parents listened to an explanation of the Project. The conversation took place on the wooden porch which apparently was not able to hold the weight, and it collapsed! The home teacher was asked to come back the next week and, possibly because there was no longer a front porch, she was invited into the house where she met and screened Joey. Based on the assessment it was determined that Joey was functioning at the "trainable" level. After some discussion, the parents agreed to participate in the Project and work with the child.

There were instances when the home teacher had to teach the mother the skill before the mother could teach it to her son. Sometimes the learning occurred simultaneously. For example, this mother and son learned to name primary colors, and both were equally proud of their accomplishments.

Because an activity chart would be of no use to this family, the home teacher relied heavily on demonstrating the teaching process necessary to implement each prescription, and on parent modeling. Recording was done on masking tape that was taped on the kitchen table with one piece of tape representing each day of the week. Hash marks were drawn on the tape which indicated to the mother the number of times the activity was to be practiced. The mother circled a hash mark for each correct response. Two older siblings were interested in the activities so the home teacher involved them in the teaching process too.

After one year in the project, Joey was the first child in this family of eight who was able to enter kindergarten. Testing data indicated he was functioning within the normal range.

Parents Who Do Not Work With Their Child Between Home Visits. Annie, the target child, was especially low in language skills and so the home teacher wanted to acquaint the mother (this was a single parent home) with the importance of verbalizing to the child.

Figure 23
Activity Sheet

PORTAGE PROJECT

Child's Name _Lonnie_

Home Teacher's Name _Helen_

Week of _December 10th_

BEHAVIOR:

Lonnie will sit self supporting without using hands for balance for 3 seconds.

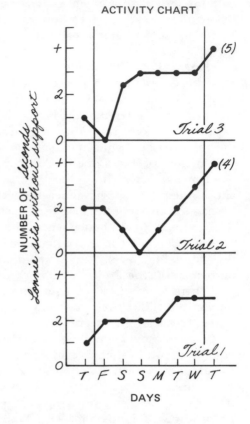

ACTIVITY CHART

NUMBER OF seconds Lonnie sits without support

DAYS

DIRECTIONS:

1. Sit on the floor with Lonnie between your legs. Rather then let Lonnie rest against your stomach, place your hand against the small of her back.

2. Give her a special toy like the "Busy Box" to play with. When she appears to be supporting herself, reduce the pressure on her back.

3. Count the number of seconds she maintains that position without using her hands (putting them on your leg) without back support.

4. Talk to her as she sits.

5. Practice 5 times/day, but just record first 3 trials.

The first prescription was, "Mom will read a story, five minutes in length, to Annie each day." The parent could simply record on the activity chart, "yes" she did read, or "no" she didn't. When the mother still hadn't accomplished the task two weeks later, the home teacher had to think of a system to motivate the mother to read to the child.

The prescription was modified the following week so that the mother would read a short story to the child daily. The home teacher put each story book in an envelope which also contained a small present for the mother, such as a comb or a small vial of perfume. She hoped that the present would motivate the mother to open the envelope, although this was no guarantee she would read to the child.

The home teacher began thinking of another kind of reinforcer for the mother. She knew that the home was lacking in many modern conveniences, like running water. To get water, the mother had to walk one mile every week with a sled or a wagon, depending on the weather, to a nearby tavern which was the closest water supply.

The real payoff was to come at the next home visit. The home teacher told the mother that if Annie could recall two facts about each of the stories that had been read to her that she, the home teacher, would get the water for the mother that week. The mother worked with the child that week and Annie could recall the facts. The best thing that happened from our point of view was that the mother was so reinforced by her child's success that she no longer needed to be coaxed into working with her child. Three weeks later, the mother said, "It's okay now. You don't have to get my water. I want to work with Annie."

Parents Who Do Not Record.   Although all the parents need to do is record the total number of correct responses on the activity chart, there are so many parents that do not record during the first month of the program years that a single example would not be instructive. However gadgets like clickers, golf counters, and knitting counters are especially helpful. Even though none of the parents' data are used to add to or modify prescriptions (baseline and post-baseline data collected by the home teacher determines that), the data can serve as a major motivator for the parents because they can see small gains that might otherwise go unnoticed. Extra praise and attention from the home teacher or staying for an extra cup of coffee have been used as a reward for the parent who records. In one case the home teacher had been trying, unsuccessfully, to get the parent to record and the parent had been trying, unsuccessfully, to get the teacher to buy panty hose. They came to a mutual satisfactory trade off—recording data for panty hose.

Some "How To's" of Working With Parents

The Project has learned several important lessons, some of them the hard way, as they relate to working with parents. A few of these suggestions are directly related to working in homes. However, most would be applicable regardless of the instructional setting.

Set Weekly Curriculum Goals.   Choosing the goals and writing the prescriptions are the most difficult tasks the teacher faces, and probably the most important. In planning individualized goals for a child and the parents, it is important that the chosen goal be one that can be achieved within one week. There may be times that this goal will not be met; however, it is extremely important that successes occur frequently and quickly, especially in the beginning. When the child succeeds, the parents succeed since they are the ones who are doing the teaching.

At this point the teacher knows from the assessment that the child, among other things, is not toilet trained, doesn't feed himself, has temper tantrums, doesn't imitate sounds, can't sort primary colors and can't hop. Where to begin? Begin where he is— with what he can already do. It really does help to look at the things the child can do, rather than the things he can't. He does stay dry for one and a half hours; he can hold a spoon, dip it and get it to his mouth with help; he does make vowel sounds and some consonant sounds spontaneously; he can sort blue plastic cars from blue plastic spoons; and he does respond to praise and smiles. Now, what could be appropriate beginning objectives that are likely to be achieved within a week? Here are a few possibilities:

- The family members will take Johnny into the bathroom with them, and they will model toileting behaviors.
- The mother will place Johnny on the toilet every one and a half hours for no more than five minutes. If Johnny performs appropriately, he will be given praise and a happy face sticker to put on the bathroom door.
- The mother will put Johnny in training pants during the day (not diapers).
- Johnny will sort blue plastic cars and yellow plastic spoons into two groups.

- Johnny will dip his spoon into sticky cereal (oatmeal) without help, will hold spoon without help, and will guide spoon to mouth with minimum aid (slight pressure on his elbow).
- The mother will count the number of tantrums Johnny has each day (baseline information).
- The mother will imitate any sound Johnny makes, and she will count the number of times Johnny imitates her.
- Johnny will stand on one foot without support for five seconds.

The choice of activities would depend totally on our mythical Johnny. He determines the curriculum. The choice, in the beginning, should be based as much on the likelihood of success as on the importance of the skill.

Show the Parent What to Do and How to Do it.   In teaching any new skill, it is important to model the behavior that is expected. For instance, in teaching a child to sort colors, a teacher wouldn't say, "Okay Johnny, sort colors." The teacher would show him what to do by doing it first. Adults being taught new skills also learn better when given concrete examples. For instance, a parent is much more likely to deal with tantrums in a certain way if shown how to do it rather than being told how to do it. This means that the teacher may have to instigate a temper tantrum and then show the parents how to handle it. The teacher finds out what typically sets Johnny off and then creates the same situation. If the technique suggested by the home teacher doesn't work, something else is tried until a technique is found that does work. In this way a technique that will work is discovered and the parents are not frustrated for a week by trying something that doesn't work. Teachers need not be afraid of trying and failing in front of the parents. The teacher is showing the parents that it is alright to make mistakes as long as the prescription is modified to achieve success. The teacher, then, is modeling problem-solving behavior for the parents. The moral then is: there is always a solution.

Have the Parents Practice Teaching the Skill.   The purpose of the home visit is to instruct the parents to teach the child, and one condition necessary for learning is the opportunity to practice. After the parents have seen the teacher work with the child and succeed, they need to experience the same success. There is a major difference in seeing an activity being taught and doing it yourself. Parents need to know they can teach effectively too in the presence of the teacher. Thus, parents will be more likely to carry out the activity when the teacher is not there. Also this provides an opportunity for the home teacher to spot problems quickly. For example, the parent might not let the child know when he is correct, or the parent might be giving too many cues or not enough. If these problems can be corrected before the teacher leaves, then the likelihood that the parents and child will succeed with the activity during the week is greatly increased.

Reinforce the Parents.   Another condition necessary to learn new skills is reinforcement. Just as the child is more likely to perform actions that are reinforced, so are the parents. Let them know; tell them when they're doing it right and be patient. It is not reasonable to expect perfection from parents. Sometimes the parent may have to break long-established behavior patterns of his own to be able to apply good techniques in teaching his child. For example, the parent may be used to doing things for the child that he can do for himself, ignoring "good" behaviors and attending to "bad" ones, or not talking to the child because he never responds anyway. It does take time, practice, and reinforcement to change old patterns, and parents should be praised for small improvements. Small improvements lead to big ones!

Individualize for Parents.   Some parents have experienced so much failure when trying to work with their child in the past, that they do not want to try again. To change this "I give up" attitude to an "I did it!" attitude may mean that the home teacher must offer parents more tangible encouragements than praise. In one home, for example, the teacher and parent drank a beer together and socialized after the home visit if the child had accomplished the skill. (It was the home teacher's last visit of the day!)

This rather atypical example serves to show that in the beginning, praise alone may not be enough to motivate some parents. However, once parents see that they can succeed and that their child can learn as a result of their teaching, you can substitute praise for the more tangible reinforcers. Success is the greatest reinforcer of all, but in some cases extraordinary measures need to be taken just to get the parents involved so they can experience success.

Involve the Parents in Planning.   As the parents experience success in teaching their child, the home teacher should reduce her help and involve the parents in planning weekly goals. Thus, the parents do not become dependent on the teacher but become confident and self-reliant in planning the curriculum for their child as well as teaching it. Some parents will reach this stage six months after they begin in the program, and some after six years. The parents should be encouraged to take as much responsibility as they can, but the home teacher should always be ready to give support, reinforcement, help, and encouragement based on the parent's needs.

Evaluation of Parent Participation

There are several ways to measure the degree of parent participation. One is to measure the progress of the children. One of the most traditional ways to do this is to compare I.Q. scores. The average I.Q. of the children in the project was 75 as determined by standardized intelligence tests. Therefore, it would be expected that on the average, the normal rate of growth would be 75 percent of that of the child with normal intelligence. One would expect that the average gain would be about six months in an eight month period of time. However, the average child in the project gained fifteen months in an eight month period. Although the home teachers did help the parents plan the curriculum, these gains in I.Q. could only have been attained through parental teaching.

Another way to evaluate the parents' effectiveness is to test the child after the summer vacation since the program does not operate during the summer months. Children who are too young to go to public school and remain in the project longer than one year are retested in September, and these test results are compared to the scores achieved the previous May. In the past there has been no significant difference in the scores although some regression might have been expected. This indicates that the parents continued to work with the child and reinforce him even though the home teacher was no longer making visits.

Ninety children were served by the Project in 1973–74 and the frequency of parental recording over that year's period of time was ninety-two percent. An average of one hundred and twenty-eight prescriptions were written per child over a year's period of time. The children were successful on ninety-one percent of the prescriptions written. This indicates that the parents taught the children during the week, and that, based on post-baseline data taken by the teacher, the children did indeed learn.

The success of this model also can be measured by the ability of parents to plan curriculum without assistance. Approximately 60 percent of the parents have been able to plan curriculum fully and write up activity charts without teacher assistance.

Furthermore, we have found that a significant number of parents are using the teaching techniques learned from the home teacher to change the behavior of other family members, in addition to the targeted child's.

The Project has attempted to conduct surveys about the Project after the program year ended to determine if a relationship existed between amount of gains made by the children and the parents' attitudes. However, the parents' comments were so positive that no relationship could be drawn (Peniston, 1972).

We think that one of the most significant informal evaluations of our project was the fact that the parents fought so hard to make sure it was funded. Three years ago (before mandatory legislation was enacted in Wisconsin) federal funds were discontinued for the direct service component of the Project. In order for the program to continue, financial support from local public school districts was necessary. Most school boards were eager for program continuation and contracted with the agency for service. Where there were exceptions, parents organized on their own and went to school board meetings requesting program continuation. They apparently were quite influential since four districts in question did opt to purchase the program. (One father told a school board that if the district didn't buy a contract for the Project, he would move his family to a school district that would!)

Final Comments Regarding the Portage Home-Based Program. This model depends upon a structured, concentrated interaction between the home teacher, the parents, and the child. It is important to be task-oriented during the home visit. There is much teaching to do, yet there is usually some time left for having a cup of coffee and socializing. During this time a parent may talk about marital, financial and other personal problems, and the home teacher can, and should, refer the parent to agencies or people who are trained to help. The teacher's expertise is in teaching—not social work, counseling, psychology, or psychiatry—but it is her responsibility to be aware of community resources that can serve these other needs. It then must be the parent's decision to contact or not to contact the suggested sources. The option and decision must be left with the parents.

Each teacher should set up a scheduled day and time for the home visit. If there is a change, parents should be informed. Because a family may have a handicapped child or may be in need of assistance does not mean the family must forfeit their right to privacy.

The teaching staff may see homes and family life styles very different from their own. Thus, it is vital for the teachers to realize and accept that they are in the homes to aid the parents to learn teaching skills and not to change life styles or value systems. The teacher should remember that he or she is a guest in each home and can only maintain the child-parent-teacher relationship with the parent's consent.

Many educators have, for too long, usurped the parent's role of responsibility in education. This condition may be magnified as more states lower the age for mandatory education for handicapped children by providing early intervention as soon as a problem is identified. Parents of the children being served need guidance and support from teachers but it is equally as important to realize and accept that teachers need parental support and guidance if the children are to achieve, maintain and increase behavioral competence.

The type of program which stimulates direct involvement of parents in teaching their children can provide parents with necessary skills and techniques to become more effective in doing what they already do and being what they already are—the single most important individuals in their child's life—his parents and teachers.

The parent-teacher relationship is one built on mutual respect and need for what each can bring to the child. This relationship with the parents and families may well be one of the most satisfying and rewarding that a teacher will ever experience.

Bibliography

Alpern, G., & Boll, T. *Developmental Profile.* Indianapolis: Psychological Development Publications, 1972.

Frohman, A., & Schortinghuis, N. "A Comparison of Professional and Paraprofessional Success with Preschool Children." *Journal of Learning Disabilities,* in press.

Peniston, E. *An Evaluation of the Portage Project.* Unpublished manuscript, The Portage Project, Cooperative Educational Agency #12, Portage, Wisconsin, 1972.

Shearer, M., & Shearer, D. The Portage Project: A Model for Early Childhood Education. *Exceptional Children,* 1972, 36, 210–217.

Shearer, D., Billingsby, J., Frohman, S., Hillard, J., Johnson, F., & Shearer, M. *Portage Checklist and Curriculum Guide to Early Education.* Portage, Wisconsin: Cooperative Educational Service Agency #12, 1972.

A Parent-Implemented Preschool Program

Ron Wiegerink
Vince Parrish

Rationale

There are several substantial reasons for involving consumers, namely parents, in service delivery systems for handicapped children. To identify a few: (1) parents know their own children best and this knowledge can be used to good advantage by others working with the children; (2) often parents spend more time with their children than do others and this time can be used to work with their children in a manner consistent with the center's goals; (3) parents can be of significant help to one another in that they share similar problems and can identify with and support one another; (4) parents can provide the project staff with ongoing evaluative feedback which can assist the program in being accountable and in making programmatic decisions; (5) parents can provide child behavioral data that can be used to monitor intervention effectiveness; (6) parents supply a source of manpower not readily available from other sources.

Each of these points is worth elaborating upon and most of them have been explored by other authors (Ora & Reisinger, 1971).

RONALD WIEGERINK is Director of the Developmental Disabilities/Technical Assistance System (DD/TAS) at the University of North Carolina in Chapel Hill. His specialties include early language development, social development, and the effectiveness of special education.

VINCE PARRISH is the Principal of the Regional Intervention Program in Nashville, Tennessee. His specialties include consumer implementation and evaluation of human service programs and parent training.

Clearly, there are not sufficient preschool services for handicapped children. Even though services have increased rapidly since the Handicapped Children's Early Education Assistance Program (HCEEP) came into being, it will be decades before all preschool handicapped children are provided with early assistance and education at the rate services are currently expanding. There are many reasons for this state of affairs: two principal reasons are a lack of financial resources to provide programs for all handicapped children and a lack of trained personnel. To accelerate the provision of services more rapidly, programs are needed which provide quality services for handicapped children at low costs and do not rely completely on professionally trained practitioners for all or even a majority of the intervention services. Currently, programs funded by the HCEEP (Handicapped Children's Early Education Program) are averaging over $3,000 per child served, with a ratio of fewer than six children served for the equivalent of each full-time, professionally trained staff member. While these costs in terms of money and manpower are not too great for a society to spend to assist handicapped children, at present our society is not willing to make these kinds of resources available to serve all handicapped children. Therefore, professionally trained persons who have the responsibility for providing services for all handicapped children must develop and implement service systems which are likely to provide quality services with substantially lower financial and human resources.

Parents are one source of such human resources. They are readily available. They are already engaged in preparing and teaching their children and are eager to learn more effective ways to rear their children and prepare them to live in society.

A project that recognized this human resource early in its inception is the Regional Intervention Program of Nashville, Tennessee. This program was one of the first group of projects funded by the Bureau of Education for the Handicapped under the Handicapped Children's Early Education Program in 1969.

The Regional Intervention Program, or RIP as it is called, was described by its first director as "a social experiment in which an agency of people, the Tennessee Department of Mental Health, in cooperation with Peabody College and the Nashville Junior League, provides the citizens of the state with a permanent organizational structure, with support for that structure, and with continuity of information within that structure, but the citizens themselves implement the organization to provide services to their children to their own satisfaction." (Ora, 1972).

The program serves developmentally disabled and behaviorally disordered preschool children from birth to age five from a twenty-six county mental health catchment area. Children and their families are referred to RIP by mental health centers, pediatricians, general practitioners, public health nurses, welfare workers, parents and other agencies when the family is no longer able to cope with the behavior and learning problems of the child. The time between contact with the project and the beginning of service to the family ranges in most cases from twenty minutes to forty-eight hours. Thus, RIP is a flexible service system always ready to admit additional families on a no-reject basis. If the family feels it can profit from the services of the program, it is always admitted.

The decision to become this flexible has meant that RIP had to design a system for delivering services that is capable of readily providing for new families at any time. Although originally RIP was designed to provide service through the vehicle of professionals, the utilization of parents in the service soon became a matter of necessity and desirability. A consumer-implemented service system gradually evolved wherein consumers provide all direct service and monitoring of the program, with the support provided by six professionally trained special educators. Designed and implemented as such, it is possible for the project staff (made up of parents and professionals) to provide comprehensive services for approximately fifty additional families during each year of operation. Comprehensive services include transportation, intake, parent training, individual tutoring, preschool classrooms, day care for siblings, medical and behavioral consultation, home visits, liaison with the social service agencies, placement and follow-along. Through these services, RIP's one objective is to prepare the family and the child for the child's maintenance and developmental progress outside of institutional care. This goal is realized if the child continues to make developmental progress after being placed in a regular day care program or public school classroom.

In order to meet this objective and deliver services, RIP is organizationally divided into functional modules which achieve management objectives (see Figure 24). Each module is supervised by a resource person who has had professional training, but all the services are provided by parents who have been served by RIP. The entire project is monitored and evaluated by an Evaluation Committee consisting of three parents and three consultants who are selected by the parents through procedures established by the committee. This committee meets regularly and has the responsibility for

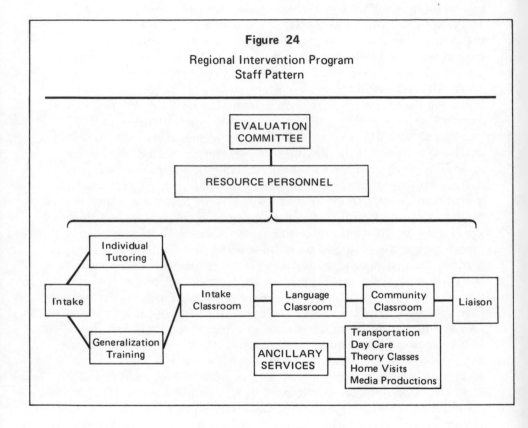

Figure 24

Regional Intervention Program
Staff Pattern

approving and generating project policies and for evaluating on-going activities. All project personnel meet with the committee at least monthly to report on module activities and individual family progress.

The committee in turn transmits a monthly report, consisting of the minutes of its meeting and its comments on the meeting, to the Department of Mental Health. The Department has perceived that such a system permits extremely close and politically astute monitoring with minimum administrative overhead.

The second level of the program is the professional resource staff which provides a middle-management function within the project. Each staff member in this level has specified areas of responsibility which are outlined by management objectives following the format of Reddin's *Effective Management by Objectives* (1971). For example, the principal of RIP is responsible for the overall administrative operations of the program. The professional staff personnel do not provide conventional special education services themselves. They work individually with parents and children only for the purposes of modeling and training, but most direct services are provided by trained parents who these resource personnel continuously consult with, train, monitor, evaluate and direct. Essentially, the professional staff members are consultants to parents responsible for the implementation of the program and providing them with expertise and personal support for planning and teaching.

The third level of the program is delivery of services which is totally parent-implemented. At this level are parents who have received training to work with their own children and have demonstrated particular expertise in at least two domains: technical and interpersonal competence. Their technical competence is, of course, constantly growing and may be in one or more of the numerous areas of project services—such as intake interviews, child assessment, classroom teaching, individual tutoring, home visits and child management. In every case, however, these consumers have demonstrated that they can operate within a management-by-objectives framework and can reliably utilize the data collection procedures of RIP. For at the center of all RIP services is the importance of objectives and data-based evaluation.

Individual factors such as personality style, interpersonal skills and interests are also considered in determining what responsibilities and functions the parent is to have. These decisions are made by the parents, who have provided the new grant with services, along with the resource personnel.

Demands for a variety of regional treatment services, constantly shifting referral patterns, and multiple funding sources over the past five years have largely determined the numbers and kinds of clients served by the RIP program. The description of the current program in terms of its clients and referral base which follows will, hopefully, be a useful referent to those interested in the evolution of the Regional Intervention Program.

Between June of 1969 and March 21, 1974, RIP served a total of 254 families. At present, approximately forty families are actively enrolled in the program with an approximate average rate of attendance of 65 percent. Thus, about twenty-six families participate in the program daily. These families have an average of 1.6 preschool children who attend RIP, bringing the program's daily attendance to approximately twenty-six adults and forty children.

The average RIP child is forty-one months old upon referral and generally will remain in the program for 8.1 months.

For the past five years, most of the referrals (76 to 80 percent) were males and approximately one-half of RIP's current referrals could be classified as seriously developmentally delayed; that is, significant delay exists in the language, motoric or cognitive areas. The remainder of the children are non-developmentally delayed, severely behaviorally disordered children who typically have been referred as "brats," oppositional, or hyperactive children.

In the first two years of operations RIP relied very heavily on local pediatricians from the Metropolitan Nashville area for referrals (in 1970-71, 76 percent of all of RIP's referrals originated from pediatricians). However, over the past three years, the pediatric referral rate has stabilized between 25 percent and 29 percent as more mental health centers, social service organizations and hospital-affiliated diagnostic clinics begin to refer to the program. Thus, the program is now fairly representative of the general population of the middle Tennessee area with 38 percent of its families in an income range below $7,000, 51 percent between $7,000 and $13,000, and 11 percent above $13,000 annual income. Further, as awareness of the program has grown, more families from rural middle Tennessee are daily attending RIP. At present, nearly 25 percent of the program's families travel more than fifty miles per day (round trip) for services and some of these commute over one hundred miles per day.

Intake

The purpose of the Intake Module is to familiarize new families with the program, to provide them with support and understanding to determine what are the next steps in providing help for the family, and to invite the parents to join if they wish. The intake process is designed to be as informal, informative, and supportive as possible. Because prescriptive diagnosis and assessment is seen as an ongoing process and an integral part of service itself, there is no need to collect complicated diagnostic data. Instead, the parent is asked simply to describe what the child does or does not do that is excessively disturbing. This information is then used to place the family in the correct service module and to identify parents who have had similiar problems and can be of help.

Following the intake interview, the parents are shown a slide show describing the program services and are then taken on a tour of the program. It is explained that parents are expected to devote from six to nine hours a week at the program working with their children. However, once a prescriptive program has been designed and implemented for them and their child is making steady progress, they are expected to commit themselves to an additional six months of volunteer work with the project helping others like themselves.

From talking to others who are working, prospective parents, they discover that most parents enjoy working after their child's intensive training needs are met because they perform newly acquired functions that give them a sense of satisfaction and accomplishment. To most parents, the opportunity to acquire talents and abilities they may not even have known they had provides an outlet for self-expression. Also, many of the parents have realized that the program's objectives of helping people to help their children and each other reflect their own values and beliefs. Only after the parents have had a chance to acquire all the information they need does the family make a decision about whether or not to participate in the program. As soon as they join, usually within an hour or so of arriving, case responsibility passes from the Intake Module to a Training Module. The coordinator, who directs the Training Module, immediately assigns other parents who are successfully dealing with similar problems to provide support to the new family until they begin to make friends on their own. A training schedule which usually begins the next day is set up for the child. If the family has other needs, the Training Module coordinator alerts support modules. In consultation with the resource personnel the Intake Coordinator can immediately activate a massive effort from teams of trained workers as well as educational, medical and social services. By the end of the morning, the family has a list showing who to call for what and what to do next. More important, they realize that they are no longer alone. People like themselves whom they can trust are using a carefully designed system to help them.

Direct Services

The family and child are then placed in a Service Module, either the Individual Tutoring or Generalization Training Module and a Classroom Module. The first two modules are designed to develop individual programs for the parent and child, and the Classroom Modules provide the child with group learning experiences and his parents with group teaching experiences.

A child unable to communicate appropriately is assigned first to the Individual Tutoring Module. The Individual Tutoring Module's goals are to produce functional speech or other adaptive behavior in the child and to instruct the parents about how to develop these skills in their own child at home. Training begins at the child's present level of development. For instance, it may start with getting him to look at people, to follow instructions, to imitate motions, sounds or words, or to recognize and name things.

In Individual Tutoring rooms the child's mother begins by learning to record which stimuli are presented to the child and how many correct responses he or she makes. Within a few daily sessions the parent becomes the teacher as well as the pupil. The parent presents the training stimuli to the child and reinforces correct responses, teaches the child at home every day and records the child's responses on a data sheet. All program training is designed solely to teach the parents what to do at home. The parent comes in daily to the Individual Tutoring Module to demonstrate progress made in the home program and to confer with the case manager on procedures as determined by the parent's and the child's needs. Individual tutoring experiences such as imitation and speech training are used because they have been repeatedly found to be an effective method of teaching parents. Once skilled in these procedures, most parents can, after a little demonstration, not only teach skills like toileting and dressing, but abide very well by the program's rule for generalization of learning: "Any desirable behavior that the child learns anywhere is thereafter required and reinforced everywhere."

Some families who enter the program do not go into the Individual Tutoring Module because they have other kinds of problems. The Generalization Training Module is designed to take care of these problems. They seek help because their child has brought

them near collapse with severe tantrums, constant crying, whining, and general unmanageability. The child may have upset meals,
refused to go to bed, abused himself, his parents, his brothers and
sisters, and his pets; destroyed things in the home; or defied all
attempts by his parents to discipline him.

Assigned to the Generalization Training Module, these families
soon learn that the problem does not reside solely in the child.
Research has shown that such behavioral disorders in toddlers are
acute and interactive, and unless help is given at any early age, such
children are in for serious problems.

In this module, training for parents and child takes place during a twenty-minute structured play session, which is designed to
elicit bad behavior from the child. The parent is instructed to request the child to change toys every two minutes. The parent-child
interaction is analyzed by continuous data recording. With the case
manager, the parent follows a manual of instructions and videotapes which teach the parents how to assume increasing responsibility for operating the module. As in all the training modules,
procedures are primarily designed to teach the parents what to do
at home.

In most cases the parent's request for the child to change toys
every two minutes results in a considerable amount of oppositional
behavior including screaming, throwing objects, sulking, and general unmanageability. Parents often respond to this behavior with
almost constant attention as they try to get the child to conform,
thus, inadvertently reinforcing the inappropriate behaviors. After
baselines on the parent and child behavior are established, parents
are taught to ignore inappropriate behaviors and praise and reinforce appropriate behavior. These procedures normally result in significant increase in praise from the parent and sharp decreases in
oppositional behavior from the child. Within a three or four week
period most parents are taught new and successful child management skills.

While the family is being served in one of these modules they
are also assigned to a classroom. Both parent and child begin in the
Intake Preschool. In addition, if the family has other preschool children who do not have day care, they are included in the classroom
programs.

The Intake Preschool does not have responsibility for the
family; responsibility always rests with only one module at a time.
Nonetheless, the Intake Preschool is a major training center for both
parent and child. Again, a standard training manual is used by the
mothers. When the parent has demonstrated that he or she can

accurately record a number of dimensions of teacher and child behavior in group situations, the parent and child advance from the
Intake Preschool. Continuous data recording shows when the
child's behavior is acceptable for one of three other preschools. One
preschool is for tiny tots and toddlers who function at the same
level. The curriculum is built around developing gross and fine
motor skills and saying single words. Another preschool is lan-
guage-oriented and these children are usually involved in individual tutoring. However, some brothers and sisters or children
from the generalization training module are included as language
models. The Language Preschool works very closely with the Individual Tutoring Module. Unlike any of the other modules related to
group activities, the Language Preschool sometimes assumes responsibility for a family, especially when the primary objective is to
provide extensive language stimulation so that the child can enter a
classroom in the community.

The third preschool is a class designed to be like those the
children will encounter in the community. Teacher-pupil ratios are
lower here than in other preschools, and social experiences are
stressed. As in all the Program's preschools, however, the child is
still on an individualized course of instruction; however, he receives less individual attention than in the other preschools. The
child's progress is evaluated on a day-to-day basis by recording
behavior and comparing it with instructional objectives. The resulting information is monitored by the child's parents, by the teachers
and the resource personnel, and by the personnel of the Liaison
Module who, at this point, take over responsibility for the family.
As the child proves to be ready for return to community schools,
the issue of an appropriate match between family and community
services arises. The Liaison personnel already have records on the
child from the Program's own community preschool, and maintain
an empirically evaluated listing of placements appropriate for various children. They investigate possible placements and consult
with the parents about the most appropriate placement. When the
child moves on to another primary educational system, the Liaison
personnel (who are a group of parents that help as they are needed)
provide support and consultation to the new teacher. They may
actively assist a teacher in programming for a child placed in her
class.

Also, should the family encounter further difficulties, the
Liaison personnel are the link to the support or intervention systems needed. All the families going back to community services
know they can obtain help from the program if they have problems.

Conversely, the program does not hesitate to call on its ever-growing network of parents throughout the region for temporary assistance.

Parent Training

In RIP, parent training and project services are the same; the entire project is designed to help parents help themselves and other parents. Parents are first taught to collect data systematically, using baseline and multiple baseline recording procedures. Data for the purposes of tutoring their child and of evaluating child progress in the preschool classrooms is collected by them. Next, parents are taught the essential skills of behavior modification, reinforcement, timing, shaping, fading, stimulus selection, and programming. As they demonstrate their behavior competencies, they begin to receive instruction in the general theories of behaviorism as presented by Skinner (1953) and Bijou & Baer (1961). They then learn more about child development primarily focusing on language development, but also they learn about social and motor development.

Once their child is making steady progress and parents have demonstrated competency in some of their basic skills, they begin to offer volunteer services which can be the beginning of a new career for some. If the parents have demonstrated mastery in individual tutoring or generalization training, they can begin as assistants in these modules. If they showed interest in one of the preschool classrooms, they could begin an assistantship there. In some cases, the parents teach others to collect basic behavioral data, but if they show programming and decision-making competencies they can take on more and more responsibilities in one of the service modules.

In most cases parents finish their six months of volunteer service and leave the service-giving aspects of the program but some stay on with the program. In some cases they serve as volunteer assistants but in cases where particular skills and interests are shown, they may become paid employees responsible for a service module such as the Intake Preschool. In some few cases, having demonstrated a good understanding of all functions of RIP, they would take on more responsibilities such as directing the Intake or Liaison Modules or being responsible for parent coordination and assignment. Some of these parents may become members of the Evaluation Committee, or may, with the additional professional training, become full-time resource personnel. Within the program all parents learn important and valuable competencies which they have an opportunity to use continuously in positions of their own choice.

Evaluation

There are three types of evaluation performed by the RIP staff: individual child progress evaluation, group or module evaluation, and project evaluation. Data are the basis for all decision-making in the program. The success of programmatic intervention is dependent upon valid and reliable data. Therefore, RIP places substantial emphasis on training staff and parents in data-collection procedures that have been designed to measure relevant behavior with reliability.

Individual data are collected in individual tutoring, generalization training, the classrooms, and by the Liaison Module. Using baseline and multiple baseline procedures the staff observes specific behavior in various response classes such as imitations, verbal behavior, motor behavior, cooperativeness, and attending. The data are used to determine the functional effects of the intervention being employed.

Group data are collected primarily by the classroom module. In the Intake Classroom, data are collected to determine both individual and group performance on the on-task/off-task dimension. The goal for each child is to be on task 85 percent of the time or more for three consecutive days. During specified times children and tasks are observed by two independent observers. These observers scan the room at specified time intervals and independently record who is on task or off task as well as teacher attention. Percentages of on- and off-task behavior are developed after twenty minutes of classroom observation. These data are used to determine individual child progress as well as group performance as a measure of program effectiveness.

Similar data procedures are used to measure verbal behavior to determine the amount of social play and interaction in the language classroom where the goals are to increase overall expressive behavior and in the community classroom. Here, the objective is for each child to engage in cooperative play behavior at least 40 percent of the time during a free play period. The Liaison Module uses similar procedures to follow-up on children as they are placed in other settings and also to describe and evaluate other preschool programs for the purpose of cataloging potential placement settings for RIP children.

RIP is also constantly in the process of utilizing data to determine overall program effectiveness. The Evaluation Committee regularly evaluates module performance and program effectiveness. In addition, RIP has been the subject of two major evaluations. One was conducted by the research cooperative and funded by the Bureau of Education for the Handicapped. The result of this study was the designation of the Regional Intervention Program as one of twelve exemplary programs for children with behavioral problems in the nation (General Learning Corporation, 1972).

Another study was conducted at the request of RIP staff and on a subcontract basis. The goal of the study was to determine RIP's cost effectiveness as a service program. The results of the detailed cost analysis study are published by the University of Tennessee (Snider and Manning, 1973).

These figures, however, do not reflect some of the program's non-monetary benefits: (1) probable prevention of behavior problems in children born to mothers subsequent to the mothers' training at RIP; (2) development of trained volunteers who could prove useful to other community action programs; (3) improved manageability of children in public schools; (4) provision of a laboratory for testing novel approaches to keeping family life intact; (5) possible reduction in juvenile delinquency for children treated in RIP; (6) training in marketable skills for parents; and (7) possible additional tax revenues resulting from gainful employment of parents who may have been unable to work without RIP involvement.

In summary, the Regional Intervention Program is a service delivery system carefully designed to provide for, and implemented by, parents of developmentally disabled and behaviorally disordered children. It is a system which is managed by stated objectives and evaluated by data to serve the best interest of the children and parents. It is a service through which parents learn to help themselves and others like them at costs which are lower than custodial and institutional care.

Bibliography

Bijou, S. W., & Baer, D. M. *Child Development, Vol. 1: A Systematic and Empirical Theory.* New York: Appleton-Century Crofts, 1961.

General Learning Corporation. "Final Report to BEH on Grant Number OEG-0-8-743242-5656." New York: author, 1972.

Ora, J. P. "Final Report for the Regional Intervention Project for Preschoolers and Parents [grant number OEG-0-9-520320-4535 (618)]." Washington: Bureau of Education for the Handicapped, Department of Health Education and Welfare, 1972.

Ora, J. P. "The Involvement and Training of Parent and Citizen Workers in Early Education for the Handicapped and Their Implications." In J. B. Jordan and R. F. Dailey (Eds.), *Not All Little Wagons Are Red*. Arlington: Center for Exceptional Children, 1972.

Ora, J. P. & Reisinger, J. *Preschool Intervention: Behavioral Service Delivery System*. Washington: American Psychological Association, 1971.

Reddin, W. J. *Effective Management by Objectives*. New York: McGraw-Hill, 1971.

Regional Intervention Project. *Regional Intervention Program Slide Show*. Nashville: author, 1970–74.

Skinner, B. F. *Science and Human Behavior*. New York: MacMillan, 1953.

Snider, J. N., & Manning, D. *Economic Analysis of Regional Intervention Program*. Knoxville: University of Tennessee, 1973.

Part  4

The Resources for Parent

Programs:

An Annotated Bibliography

Introduction

Art Cross

The entries in this bibliography are intended to allow the reader to augment his knowledge of the information discussed in Parts 2 and 3 of this book. The bibliography is not exhaustive. The listings that have been included were selected because they contained diverse (general or research) information which would prove applicable to several areas of a parent program.

Since many of the references pertain to more than one of the six areas in the list below, a key has been included at the end of each title listing to direct the reader to the citations most appropriate to his needs.

1. Social-Emotional Support
2. Information Exchange
3. Parent-Child Interaction
4. Parent Participation
5. Training
6. Planning

ART CROSS is a Research Assistant at the Frank Porter Graham Child Development Center at the University of North Carolina in Chapel Hill. His interests include young handicapped children and their families, staff development, and the organizational and social aspects of interaction.

Bibliography

Art Cross
Patricia F. Weiss

Aaronson, M. and Rosenfeld, J. *Baby and Other Teachers.* Washington: Day-Care and Child Development Council, 1973.   **3**

An interesting cartoon character format describing the emotional and educational needs of babies and the emotional relationships within the family. The authors include an excellent list of annotated references on child development and parent-child relationships.

* Day Care and Child Development Council of America
1012 14th Street, N.W.
Washington, D.C. 20005 ($2.25)

Adair, T. and Eckstein, E. *Parents and the Day Care Center.* New York: Federation of Protestant Welfare Agencies, 1969.   **6**

Parent participation is discussed in terms of parents as "actual and potential assets, capable of helping the center toward a mutual widening of horizons." Attention is given to developing a parent-group profile, a community profile, and channels of communication for more accurate assessment of parental needs for involvement. The last pages are devoted to evaluation questions.

Federation of Protestant Welfare Agencies
281 Park Avenue, South
New York, New York 10010 ($1.65)

PATRICIA F. WEISS is a Research Assistant at the Technical Assistance Development System in Chapel Hill. Her main area of interest is learning disabilities in preschool, emotionally disturbed children.

* Information on availability of materials in this bibliography is accurate as of January 1976.

Ahr, A. and Simons, B. *Parent Handbook: Developing Your Child's Skills and Abilities at Home.* Skokie, Illinois: Priority Innovations, Inc., 1968.   **3**

A guide for parents who wish to influence their child's behavior so that the child is prepared for school entry. The book contains ideas and activities for working with children in the following areas: comprehension, developing the senses, language, concepts, motor coordination, auditory discrimination, and visual memory.

Priority Innovations, Inc.
P. O. Box 792
Skokie, Illinois 60076 ($2.25)

Auerbach, A. (in cooperation with Child Study Associations of America) *Parents Learn Through Group Discussion: Principles and Practices of Parent Group Education.* New York: John Wiley and Sons, Inc., 1968.   **4, 5, 6**

Details for planning and carrying through continuous small group discussions. This book is mainly for professionals who need guidelines for conducting groups for educating parents about handicapping conditions of children.

John Wiley and Sons
Eastern Distribution Center
1 Wiley Drive
Somerset, New Jersey 08873 ($11.95)

Baldwin, V.; Fredericks, H. D.; and Brodsky, G. *Isn't It Time He Outgrew This? or A Training Program for Parents of Retarded Children.* Springfield, Illinois: Charles C. Thomas, 1973.   **3, 5**

Specific programs for parents who want to develop certain types of behaviors in their retarded child. The parent, without prior training or consultation from professionals, should be able to implement his own specific programs and measure the progress of his child by utilizing the behavior modification techniques and basic learning principles described in this book.

Charles C. Thomas
301-327 East Lawrence Avenue
Springfield, Illinois 62717 ($8.95)

Barten, H. and Barten, S. *Children and Their Parents in Brief Therapy.* New York: Behavioral Publications, 1973.   **5, 6**

A collection of readings which brings together recent innovative strategies and illustrates a wide range of therapeutic approaches to children and their families. Emphasis in this book is on the mental health of the family setting and the relationship of family setting to the development of the child.

Human Science Press
72 Fifth Avenue
New York, New York 10011 ($13.95)

Bauch, J.; Vietze, P.; and Morris, V. "What Makes the Difference in Parental Participation?" *Childhood Education* 50 (October 1973): 47–53.   **4**

A study of data from an Alabama Head Start Project to see which factors most influence the degree of parent participation. According to the study, the most important variable was the size of the center, and the next most important variable was the efforts expended by projects to facilitate participation (i.e., baby-sitting, transportation, etc.).

Childhood Education
3615 Wisconsin Avenue, N.W.
Washington, D.C. 20402 ($2.25 for journal)

Becker, W. *Parents Are Teachers*. Champaign, Illinois: Research Press Company, 1971.   **3, 5**

An instructional book on the systematic use of consequences (reinforcers) to teach children in positive ways. The book, which is intended to help parents learn to be more effective teachers, is also useful for staff development and in-service training in behavior management techniques. Ten units with exercises and projects, as well as forms on which to keep records of the target behavior, are included.

Research Press Company
Box 3177
Champaign, Illinois 61820 ($4.00)

Bricklin, P. "Counseling Parents of Children with Learning Disabilities." *The Reading Teacher* 23 (January 1970): 331–338.   **1, 5**

A description of the parent involvement aspects of the Parkway Day School. This article gives a solid rationale for counseling as a method of alleviating parental anxiety and increasing parent-staff communication; it also gives specifics on group size, leadership, and discussions.

International Reading Association
800 Barksdale Road
Newark, Delaware 19711 ($2.00 for issue)

Brim, O. G. *Education for Child Rearing.* New York: Free Press, 1959.
2, 5, 6

A discussion of all aspects of parent education: nature of parent education; influence of parent on child; cause of parent behavior; aims and clientele of parent education; content; methods; training; and evaluation. This book is most applicable to large-scale parent-education programs.

Free Press
866 Third Avenue
New York, New York 10022 ($2.45)

Brown, C. *For Beginning-to-be-Teachers of Beginning-to-be-Students.* Nashville, Tennessee: DARCEE, George Peabody College for Teachers, 1971.
3, 5

Helpful information for adults working in a classroom on all aspects of teaching skills and "what a teacher should know." The book includes practical suggestions on content and methods of teaching: child behavior, lesson planning, discipline, parents, and evaluation.

DARCEE
Publication Office
Peabody College
Box 154
Nashville, Tennessee 37203 ($3.50)

Brown, D. *Developmental Handicaps in Babies and Young Children: A Guide for Parents.* Springfield, Illinois: Charles C. Thomas, 1972.   **2**

A guide for parents whose infants are exhibiting developmental delay. This book, which serves as a simplified overview of developmental problems and primary handicapping conditions, offers a very useful description of the benefits of complete diagnostic evaluation. A discussion of how to locate and utilize community resources and a dictionary of terms to help the layman understand the specialists' language.

Charles C. Thomas
301-327 East Lawrence Avenue
Springfield, Illinois 02717 ($5.75)

Bryan, D. *Guide for Parents of Preschool Visually Handicapped Children.* Springfield, Illinois: Illinois State Office of the Superintendent of Public Distinction, 1969.   **2, 3**

An offering of techniques in everyday care for parents of visually handicapped children. This booklet, which is a combination of suggestions from mothers and professionals, discusses parental attitudes and the child's early needs, activities and behavior, and the resources available for help and guidance.

Illinois Office of Education
100 North 1st Street
Springfield, Illinois 62777 (free)

Bryant, J. "Parent-Child Relationships: Their Effect on Rehabilitation." *Journal of Learning Disabilities* 4 (June-July 1971): 325–329.   **1, 2**

An exploration of three basic types of relationships of parents in regard to their children and their disorders: those who accept, those who reject, and those who compensate. The discussion, which revolves around the way compensation impedes rehabilitation, includes recommendations on counseling of parents of handicapped children.

Journal of Learning Disabilities
5 North Wabash Avenue
Chicago, Illinois 60602 ($ .50)

Calvert, D. "Dimensions of Family Involvement in Early Childhood Education." *Exceptional Children* 37 (May 1971): 655–659.   **6**

A consideration of how best to involve all family members in early intervention programs for handicapped children. In order to plan for maximum benefit, it is urged that the following dimensions be considered: which family members should participate, what should be the nature of their involvement, why should they participate, when should they become involved, and how can their involvement best be secured?

Information Center
Council for Exceptional Children
1920 Association Drive
Reston, Virginia 22091 (free, one copy)

Cansler, D. and Cross, A. *Helping Hands.* Durham, North Carolina: Learning Institute of North Carolina, 1975.   **4, 5, 6**

A rationale for working with families, a methodology for planning the parent program, and suggestions for activities which will foster parent-professional interaction. This booklet includes a list of other helpful books for parents and staff.

Childrens 100
LINC
1006 Lamond Avenue
Durham, North Carolina 27701 (free, single copy)

Chess, S. "The Influence of Defect on Development in Children with Congenital Rubella." *Merrill-Palmer Quarterly* 20 (1974): 225–274.   **3**

A reevaluation of children with congenital rubella initially studied at ages two to four. The article cites data which indicate individual differences in children's temperament and in the parent-child interaction affect the child's ability to master his handicap.

Merrill-Palmer Quarterly
71 East Ferry Avenue
Detroit, Michigan 48202 ($3.75, journal)

Clarke-Stewart, K. A. *Interactions Between Mothers and Their Young Children: Characteristics and Consequences.* Monographs of the Society for Research in Child Development, Vol. 38. Chicago: Univ. of Chicago Press, 1973.   **3, 5**

An examination of the relations between behaviors of mothers and children. The author reports that stimulating, responsive mothers influence the child's intellectual development, while in the area of social relations the child's behavior influences the mother's behavior; the implications for mothers' training programs are suggested.

University of Chicago Press
5801 South Ellis Avenue
Chicago, Illinois 60637 ($7.00, issue)

Cliff, S.; Gray, J.; and Nymann, C. *Mothers Can Help . . . A Therapist's Guide for Formulating a Developmental Text for Parents of Special Children.* El Paso, Texas: El Paso Rehabilitation Center, 1974.   **2, 3, 5, 6**

An information handbook for groups of mothers of young children (six months to three years) who have developmental delays. The book is designed: (1) to instruct mothers in methods that will aid all areas of their child's development and (2) to aid mothers in adjusting to and accepting their handicapped child. In addition to activities for all developmental areas (motor, language, emotional), there are three additional chapters that are especially helpful: "Developmental Play," "Influencing Child Behavior," and "Family Relationships."

El Paso Rehabilitation Center
2630 Richmond
El Paso, Texas 79930 ($9.50)

Cole, A., et al. *Recipes for Fun.* Winnetta, Illinois: Parents as Resources, 1970.   **3, 5**

A booklet written on the premise that parents are key figures in developing their child's intelligence, creativity, and awareness of the world. The booklet, which points out to parents things they can do to utilize this potential, is divided into hints (what to save, what to buy), make-believe activities, music and rhythm, making things, exploring, learning games and party fun. It emphasizes using articles already available in the home and learning by doing.

Bar Projects
464 Central Avenue
Northfield, Illinois 60093 ($2.50)

Davis, F. *Passage Through Crisis: Polio Victims and Their Families.* Indianapolis: Bobbs-Merrill, 1963.   1

A sociological inquiry into the problems of families when a child contracts polio. This book is a good presentation of the "identity stresses" of both the child and the family; discussed are the various perceptual modifications which take place when there is the realization that something is wrong. Other issues dealt with are "the shift in family image, the problem of ambiguous communications from the doctor; expectations for improvement and adjustment strategies of the parents."

Bobbs-Merrill
4 West 58th Street
New York, New York 10019 ($3.50)

Dittman, L. *The Infants We Care For.* Washington, D.C.: National Association for the Education of Young Children, 1973.   5, 6

A description of operational considerations in centers and home-based programs for infants and toddlers which includes chapters by White, Brazelton, Provence, Huntingdon and others. The author offers an excellent rationale and goals for working with families, selection of staff, and programmatic options.

National Association for the Education of Young Children
1834 Connecticut Avenue, N.W.
Washington, D.C. 20009 ($2.00)

Donahue, M., et al. *Parent Discussion Manual.* Marshalltown, Iowa: Marshall-Powenshiek Joint County School System, 1973.   4, 5

A professional guide to a parent education course for mental stimulation of handicapped children. The manual is organized on the basis of the topics of twelve sessions: orientation, responsive program, toys as learning tools, creativity, self-concept, discipline, behavior modification I and II, language, sensory motor development I and II, and open session.

Area Education Agency #6
Preschool Division
507 East Anson
Marshalltown, Iowa 50158 ($6.00)

Education Resource Information Center/Early Childhood Education Newsletter.
2, 6

A quarterly published by the ERIC Clearinghouse on Early Childhood Education. Offers up-to-date information on research studies, current issues, and programs for children aged birth to twelve.

Publications Office
College of Education, University of Illinois
805 West Pennsylvania Avenue
Urbana, Illinois 61801 ($2.00, four issues)

Ehlers, W. *Mothers of Retarded Children: How They Feel, Where They Find Help.* Springfield, Illinois: Charles C. Thomas, 1966. 1, 6

Documentation of interviews with twenty-four mothers of severely retarded children. Included is information on how the mothers perceived the retardation, how they made decisions in seeking and using help, and how they reacted to and valued the services rendered. Information is also given on (1) the children, the families, and the service program, (2) the mothers, and (3) the services of the clinic. A useful bibliography is also included.

Charles C. Thomas
301-327 East Lawrence Avenue
Springfield, Illinois 62717 ($6.75)

Exceptional Children. 41 (May 1975). 5, 6

A special issue titled "The Parent-Professional Partnership" in which all articles pertain to aspects of parent involvement. Articles include the following: "On Being the Parent of a Handicapped Child," "A Lost Generation of Parents," "Matching Families and Services," "Mothers of Retarded Children Review a Parent Education Program," and "The Brain-Damaged Parent (A Parody on Special Services)."

Information Center
Council for Exceptional Children
1920 Association Drive
Reston, Virginia 22091 (free, one copy)

Exceptional Children Conference Papers: Parent Participation in Early Childhood Education. Reston, Virginia: Council for Exceptional Children, 1969.
5, 6

A discussion of the following areas: (1) dimensions of family involvement, (2) relationship of parent, child and professional, (3) parent reactions to identification of handicaps, (4) parent participation in behavior modification for physically handicapped children, (5) the use of parent meetings and parent educators, (6) programs for training mothers to instruct their infants at home, (7) sociological perspectives on parent counseling, and (8) early diagnosis of deafness and parent counseling.

ERIC Document Reproduction Service
P. O. Box 190
Arlington, Virginia 22210 ($6.00)
request EDO 34910

The Exceptional Parent. Boston: Psy-Ed Corporation. 2

Practical information for parents of children with all kinds of handicaps on day-to-day care and long range planning. A few of the topics covered are professional information without professional jargon, on key issues such as psychological testing, visits to the dentist, things to make for parents and kids, general discussions of disabilities, and a parent forum with questions and answers from parents. This magazine is a forum for the mutual sharing of information by parents and professionals concerned with handicapped children.

Exceptional Parent
Subscription
P. O. Box 964
Manchester, New Hampshire 03105 ($10.00, one year)

Faragher, J.; Garskof, B.; and Hoffnung, M. *Parent Cooperative Group Child Care.* Urbana, Illinois: University of Illinois, 1975. 6

A rationale for the establishment of cooperative group care on a wide basis which examines historical and social dynamics affecting family structure and child care. One cooperative is described in detail.

Publications Office
College of Education, University of Illinois
805 West Pennsylvania Avenue
Urbana, Illinois 61801 ($2.50)

Farber, B. *Mental Retardation—Its Social Context and Social Consequences.* Boston: Houghton Mifflin, 1968. 6

A book on the social aspects of mental retardation which includes techniques for determining prevalence, social factors in prevalence, consequences of labeling persons as mentally retarded, the effects of and on the family, parent organizations, and the structure of residential institutions. Farber regards the mentally retarded as a surplus population because of institutional selection processes in our society;

there are important implications which arise from being part of a surplus population.

Houghton Mifflin
2 Park Street
Boston, Massachusetts 02107 ($9.50)

Forrester, B. J., et al. *Home Visiting with Mothers and Infants.* Nashville, Tennessee: DARCEE, George Peabody College, 1971.   **3, 5, 6**

Information about a home visiting strategy for mothers and infants and home visitor practices for modifying mother's interactions with their infants. Discusses considerations that underlie the home visiting approach; overall process of planning, implementation, and evaluation; how home visiting proceeds; and suggestions, observations, and evaluation of home visits. (Is geared toward use with low-income families.)

DARCEE
Publication Office
George Peabody College
Nashville, Tennessee 37203 ($4.00)

Forrester, B. J., et al. *Materials for Infant Development.* Nashville, Tennessee: DARCEE, George Peabody College for Teachers, 1971.   **3**

A discussion of materials that promote infant growth and development. These materials are used in the DARCEE home visiting program.

DARCEE
Publication Office
George Peabody College
Nashville, Tennessee 37203 ($4.00)

Fraiberg, S. "Intervention in Infancy: A Program for Blind Infants." *Journal of the American Academy of Child Psychiatry* 10 (July, 1971).   **3, 6**

A report on longitudinal studies of the uniqueness of the developmental patterns of the blind baby. Discusses the use of home visits to show parents how to assist their infant's development.

Journal Department
Yale University Press
92 A Yale Station
New Haven, Connecticut 06520 ($6.00, journal)

Frost, J. "At Risk!" *Childhood Education* 51 (April-May, 1975): 298–304.   **6**

An overview of significant research on intervention programs for high risk infants and young children. A concrete rationale for family-oriented intervention and a discussion of how the infant socializes the mother into motherhood are offered.

Childhood Education
3615 Wisconsin Avenue, N.W.
Washington, D.C. 20402 ($2.50, journal)

Furman, R. and Katan, A. *The Therapeutic Nursery School.* New York: International University Press, 1969.   **1, 5, 6**

A description of an approach for working with emotionally disturbed preschool children utilizing the mother as therapist. This volume, which is one of the best sources available on the use of parent as therapist, gives explicit details on administrative policies, educational programs, techniques of working with the mother, and case reports. The book includes many useful appendices.

International University Press, Inc.
239 Park Avenue
New York, New York 10003 ($12.50)

Galloway, C. and Galloway, K. *Parent Groups with a Focus on Precise Behavior Management, II.* Nashville, Tennessee: Institute on Mental Retardation and Intellectual Development, Peabody College, 1970.   **4, 5**

An explanation of procedures for setting up a parent group to instruct parents of retarded children to use the tools of precision teaching in dealing with behavior problems at home. The author examines: strategies for developing parent groups; instruction of parents in the methods of precision teaching; examples of parent projects; and the question "Why do some parents participate and others don't?" This material can be used as a basis for teaching parents how to record baseline data on their child's behavior, intervene, and see if the rate of the behavior changes.

IMRID Publications
George Peabody College
Box 154
Nashville, Tennessee 37203 (free)

Giesy, R., ed. *A Guide for Home Visitors.* Nashville, Tennessee: DARCEE, George Peabody College, 1970.   **5**

A guide developed for use with paraprofessionals in the homes of low-income children, which provides information for persons who are training to be home visitors. Topics discussed include: introduction to the home visiting approach, living conditions that influence learning, how home visiting is done, and recording home visits. The appendix includes suggested activities for home visits, and a sample unit.

DARCEE
Publication Office
George Peabody College
Nashville, Tennessee 37203 ($4.50)

Gilkerson, E. *Teacher-Child-Parent Relationships.* New York: Early Childhood Education Council of New York, 1972.   **1, 2, 5**

An in-depth discussion of what is involved in mutual cooperation between teacher and parent as they focus upon the child. This booklet offers much practical advice, emphasizing the facilitation of joint, relaxed discussions of concrete situations and questions.

Early Childhood Education Council of New York
220 Waverly Place
New York, New York 10014 ($ .50)

Glasscote, R. and Fishman, M. *Mental Health Programs for Preschool Children.* Washington: Joint Information Service of the American Psychiatric Association and the National Association of Mental Health, 1974.   **6**

A collection of program descriptions of eight outstanding preschool programs around the country which emphasize the mental health aspects of working with young children and their families. This book contains an excellent overview of the emotional needs of young children and their parents; it is an excellent resource of information when considering program alternatives.

American Psychiatric Association
1700 18th Street, N.W.
Washington, D.C. 20009 ($7.00, single copy)

Goffman, E. *Stigma: Notes on the Management of Spoiled Identity.* Englewood Cliffs, New Jersey: Prentice Hall, Inc., 1963.   **1**

A discussion of stigmatized individuals: persons who do not (or can not) conform to standards which society calls normal. Some of the topics are: the way society provides the means for categorizing people; the important distinction between being discredited and being discreditable; how a stigma can be used as a "crutch" for secondary gains; how tension is managed if the stigma is easily perceived (by others); how information is managed if it is not apparent; the importance of the perceptibility and the obtrusiveness of a stigma.

Prentice Hall, Inc.
Englewood Cliffs, New Jersey 07632 ($2.45)

Gordon, I. J. and Lally, R. *Stimulation for Infants—Baby Learns Through Baby Play.* New York: St. Martin's Press, 1969.   **3**

A presentation for mother in nontechnical language on the value of "learning games." The major part of the manual is "games," presented in eight series, arranged according to development. Each game is illustrated and is explained in the following categories: position (mother and baby); action (what mother is supposed to do); arm (what the baby is to do); and purpose (why is this game useful?). The appendix includes suggestions for making toys.

St. Martin's Press
125 Fifth Avenue
New York, New York 10010 ($3.95, paper)

Gordon, T. *Parent Effectiveness Training: The "No-Lose" Program for Raising Responsible Children.* New York: Peter W. Wyden, Inc., 1971.   **5**

A description of a complete model for effective parent-child relationships. Discusses such areas as: parents as persons, active listening, putting "I-messages" to work, parental power, "no-lose" method to solve conflicts, and exercises to facilitate using the model.

David McKay Company
750 Third Avenue
New York, New York 10017 ($10.95)

Gray, S. "The Child's First Teacher." *Childhood Education* 48 (1971): 127–129.   **2, 6**

A description of the philosophy (working with the mother) behind the programs of the Demonstration and Research Center for Early Education, as well as an examination of the reasons for the success of the home visitor programs.

Childhood Education
3615 Wisconsin Avenue, N.W.
Washington, D.C. 20402 ($1.75, issue)

Green, J. S. *Parent Education Handbook.* Chattanooga, Tennessee: Tennessee Re-Education Program, Tennessee Department of Mental Health, Children's Re-Education Center, undated.   **5**

A guide based on Gordon's *Parent Effectiveness Training* for individuals who are interested in offering courses in parent education; discusses functions of group leader; structure of the parent group; areas for group discussion such as defining behaviors; contracting, punishment; teaching responsibility; and communications in the family.

Small Wood's School
Moccasin Bend Road
Chattanooga, Tennessee 37405 (free)

Grotberg, E. *Day Care: Resources for Decisions.* Washington: Day Care and Child Development Council of America, 1971.   **3, 4, 6**

> An extensive volume of information related to aspects of day care and child development. Special attention should be given to three chapters on adult involvement: Chapter 8, "Adult-Child Interaction and Personalized Day Care" by E. K. Beller; Chapter 9, "Parent Involvement in Early Education" by Robert Hess and others; and Chapter 10, "Parent-Training Programs and Community Involvement in Day Care" by Robert Hess and others.

> Day Care and Child Development Council of America
> 1012 14th Street, N.W.
> Washington, D.C. 20005 ($4.50 plus 50¢ postage)

Guerney, B. G., Jr., ed. *Psychotherapeutic Agents: New Roles for Nonprofessionals, Parents, and Teachers.* New York: Holt, Rinehart and Winston, Inc., 1969.   **5**

> A background on the historical developments and rationale for the use of nonprofessionals in meeting children's mental health needs. Emphasis is on remedial methods and procedures, and details are given on the selection, roles and methods in training nonprofessionals.

> Holt, Rinehart and Winston
> 383 Madison Avenue
> New York, New York 10017 ($11.00)

Harms, T. and Smith, J. *Changes in Parent/Teacher Expectations in Cooperative Preschools.* Urbana, Illinois: University of Illinois, 1975.   **4**

> A discussion of the sources of conflict in parent cooperatives and suggested ways to help resolve some of the conflicts.

> Publications Office
> College of Education, University of Illinois
> 805 West Pennsylvania Avenue
> Urbana, Illinois 61801 ($1.50)

Hawkins, R.; Peterson, R.; Schweid, E.; and Bijou, S. "Behavior Therapy In the Home: Amelioration of Problem Parent-child Relations with the Parent in a Therapeutic Role." *Journal of Experimental Child Psychology* 4 (September 1966): 99–107.   **3, 5**

> A detailed case study description of the operant modification of a problematic mother-child relationship. This article contains an excellent description of the use of operant techniques in training parents to alter relationships with their children.

Journal Subscription Department
Academic Press
111 Fifth Avenue
New York, New York 10003 ($34.00, volume)

Hersh, A. "Changes in Family Functioning Following Placement of a Retarded Child." *Social Work* 15 (October 1970): 93–102 **1, 6**

Case studies of fifteen families for three months after placement of their children in a residential school. The article has strong implications for preschool practices.

Publication Sales Office
49 Sheridan Avenue
Albany, New York 12210 ($4.00, volume)

Honig, A. *Language Learning, Language Development: A Bibliography.* Urbana, Illinois: University of Illinois, 1975. **3**

Citations on a wide variety of books, periodicals, papers and speeches including some ERIC documents which focus on the broad spectrum of normal development in language functioning. Includes background readings on language, curriculum, materials, and procedures for language learning programs, studies of parent and family interactions related to children's language development, and reports of language assessment.

Publications Office
College of Education, University of Illinois
805 West Pennsylvania Avenue
Urbana, Illinois 61801 ($3.50)

Honig, A. *Parent Involvement in Early Childhood Education.* Washington: National Association for the Education of Young Children, 1974. **6**

An up-to-date account of the varieties of programs which are oriented toward family involvement. Contents include: research, rights of parents, ways to increase sensitivity and skills, and an extensive list of current resources and materials.

National Association for the Education of Young Children
1834 Connecticut Avenue, N.W.
Washington, D.C. 20009 ($3.00)

Hovey, E. *Ethnicity and Early Education.* Urbana, Illinois: University of Illinois, 1975. **6**

A review of the relationship between ethnicity and early academic success which includes an examination of the rationales of several ethnic groups for the education of their young children.

Publications Office
College of Education, University of Illinois
805 West Pennsylvania Avenue
Urbana, Illinois 61801 ($1.50)

Howard, N., compiler. *Cultural and Cross Cultural Studies: An Abstract Bibliography.* Urbana, Illinois: University of Illinois, 1974.   **6**

A list of recent documents and journal articles describing cultural differences and their influence on children's cognitive, social, emotional, and language development.

Publications Office
College of Education, University of Illinois
805 West Pennsylvania Avenue
Urbana, Illinois 61801 ($2.00)

Howard, N., compiler. *Day Care: An Abstract Bibliography* (Supplement #2). Urbana, Illinois: University of Illinois, 1974.   **5, 6**

An update of a previous bibliography which includes references to both family and center day care, staff training programs, physical facilities, evaluation, and other topics.

Publications Office
College of Education, University of Illinois
805 West Pennsylvania Avenue
Urbana, Illinois 61801 ($1.50)

Howard N., compiler. *Discipline and Behavior: An Abstract Bibliography.* Urbana, Illinois: University of Illinois, 1974.   **3**

A list of recent documents and journal articles on discipline and behavior modification.

Publications Office
College of Education, University of Illinois
805 West Pennsylvania Avenue
Urbana, Illinois 61801 ($1.50)

Howard, N., compiler. *Education of Preschool and Elementary Teachers: An Abstract.* Urbana, Illinois: University of Illinois, 1974.   **5, 6**

Documents and journal articles describing various approaches to the education of teachers of young children.

Publications Office
College of Education, University of Illinois
805 West Pennsylvania Avenue
Urbana, Illinois 61801 ($2.25)

Howard, N., compiler. *Open Education: An Abstract Bibliography (Supplement #1).* Urbana, Illinois: University of Illinois, 1974.   **6**

An update of a previous ERIC bibliography on open-education and open-plan schools. Focuses on open education practices in preschool, kindergarten, and elementary school.

Publications Office
College of Education, University of Illinois
805 West Pennsylvania Avenue
Urbana, Illinois 61801 ($2.50)

Howard, N., compiler. *Regular Class Placement of the Exceptional Child: An Abstract Bibliography.* Urbana, Illinois: University of Illinois, 1974.   **6**

A list of documents and journal articles on placement of exceptional children (handicapped, gifted) in regular preschool, kindergarten, and elementary classrooms.

Publications Office
College of Education, University of Illinois
805 West Pennsylvania Avenue
Urbana, Illinois 61801 ($1.50)

Howells, J. *Theory and Practice of Family Psychiatry.* New York: Brunner/ Mazel, 1971.   **3, 6**

An extensive volume dealing with all aspects of therapy and services to the family as an ecological system. Of special interest are four major articles: "Considerations Regarding the Parent-Infant Relationship" by Phyllis Greenacre; "The Communication of Distress Between Parent and Child Relations in an Urban Culture" by Margaret Mead; and an excellent evaluative source "The Psychometric Assessment of the Family" by J.R. Lickorish.

Bruner/Mazel
64 University Place
New York, New York 10003 ($25.00)

Howlin, P., et al. "A Home-based Approach to the Treatment of Autistic Children." *Journal of Autism and Childhood Schizophrenia* 3 (October-December 1973): 308–336.   **3, 5**

A description of a treatment approach emphasizing the advantages of using parents as therapists and providing treatment at the home rather than the clinic. Stresses the need for assessment of the family as well as the child so that treatment may be individually adapted to the particular family circumstances.

Plenum Publication Corporation
227 West 17th Street
New York, New York 10011 ($10.00)

Jelinek, J. and Scraub, M. "A Model of Parent Involvement in Programming for Communicatively Handicapped Children." *Rehabilitation Literature* 34 (August 1973): 321–324.   6

A delivery approach for a rural area (Wyoming) consisting of an intensive summer program and a follow-up phase. Discusses the use of a variety of curriculum methods and materials, the development of individual instructional packets, and the coordination of programming with local professionals.

National Easter Seal Society for Crippled Children and Adults
2023 West Ogden Avenue
Chicago, Illinois 60612 ($ .15 plus postage)

Jew, W. "Helping Handicapped Infants and Their Families: The Delayed Development Project." *Children Today* 3 (May-June 1974): 7–13.   6

A description of the Delayed Development Project, a program that serves children from birth through the age of three in San Joaquin County, California. Contains information on parent involvement, community involvement, and project evaluation.

U.S. Government Printing Office
Washington, D.C. 20402 ($1.25, single issue)

Journal of Research and Development in Education: Parental Involvement (Winter, 1975).   **2, 5, 6**

Entire issue on aspects of parent involvement. Contributions include an overview by Patricia Adkins and David Lillie, several program descriptions ranging from language intervention to behavior modification, and a very pertinent cautionary article by Bernard Farber and Michael Lewis, entitled "The Symbolic Use of Parents," which questions the nature and purposes of the increase in parent programs.

Journal of Research and Development in Education
Business Manager Room 220
175 West Wieuca Road, N.E.
Atlanta, Georgia 30342 ($2.00, journal)

Kamara, B. *Developing Parent Power in the Head Start Program.* Greensboro, North Carolina: LINC Child Development Training Center, 1971.   **6**

A speech which gives insight into the difficulties that poor people have in coping with a life of poverty. It presents parent involvement from a parent's point of view.

LINC Child Development Training Center
1001 North Elm Street
Greensboro, North Carolina 27401 (free)

Karnes, M.; Studley, W.; Wright, W.; and Hodgins, A. "An Approach for Working with Mothers of Disadvantaged Preschool Children." *Merrill-Palmer Quarterly* 14 (1968): 174–184   **5, 6**

A study designed to determine the effects of short term parent training on the intellectual and language development of their preschool children.

Merrill-Palmer Publication Office
71 East Ferry Avenue
Detroit, Michigan 48202 ($ .10 per page)

Karnes, M. and Zehrbach, R. "Flexibility in Getting Parents Involved in the School." *Teaching Exceptional Children* 5 (Fall 1972): 6–19.   **4, 5, 6**

A description of a variety of strategies and techniques to meet the multiple goals of each family in a parent program, based on a needs assessment in helping parents select the desired type of involvement. Within each strategy, consideration is given to application, misapplication, advantages and disadvantages.

Colonel Wolfe School
403 East Healey Street
Champaign, Illinois 61820 (free)

Karnes, M.; Zehrback, R.; and Teska, J. "A Family Involvement Model: Implementation with Families of Multihandicapped Children." *Theory Into Practice* (June 1972): 150–156.   **5, 6**

A description of a research-based model to be used for the planning and implementation of programs for families of handicapped children. A detailed account of what is included in each of the five areas of the Model (Acquaint, Teach, Support, Expand, and Maintain) is included.

Theory Into Practice
149 Arps Hall
1945 N. High Street
Columbus, Ohio 43210 ($1.50, issue)

Kelly, E. *Parent-Teacher Interaction, A Special Education Perspective.* Seattle: Special Child Publications, 1974. **5, 6**

A collection of practical information for the classroom teacher in both general and special education. Topics include planning and implementing group meetings, dissemination of information, individual parent counseling, parental involvement in behavior management, and the instructional process.

Special Child Publications
A Division of Bernie Straub Publication Company, Inc.
4535 Union Bay Place, N.E.
Seattle, Washington 98105 ($3.90)

Kirk, S. A.; Karnes, M. B.; and Kirk, W. D. *You and Your Retarded Child.* Palo Alto, California: Pacific Books, 1968. **2, 5**

A manual for parents of retarded children which provides both information and instructional materials. Various topics which should be of interest to parents with a retarded child are discussed; there is a chapter on levels of retardation and a discussion to help answer the question, "How retarded is my child?"; there is an extensive checklist of "normal" child development with which parents can compare their own child's development; and there are good chapters dealing with self-help skills, playing, talking, and emotional adjustment.

Pacific Books
Box 558
Palo Alto, California ($5.95)

Kogan, K.; Gordon, B.; and Wimberger, H. "Teaching Mothers to Alter Interactions with Their Children: Implications for Those who Work with Children and Parents." *Childhood Education* 49 (November 1972): 107–110. **3, 5**

A summary and description of research at the Child Development and Mental Retardation Center of the University of Washington which deals with styles of social interaction between young children and their mothers. Variety of techniques are offered as adjuncts to help reinforce a mother's use of the suggested behaviors.

Childhood Education
3615 Wisconsin Avenue, N.W.
Washington, D.C. 20402 ($1.75)

Kremer, B. *Parent Education: Abstract Bibliography.* Urbana, Illinois: ERIC Clearinghouse on Early Childhood Education, 1971. **5, 6**

An annotated bibliography containing citations mostly available from ERIC. Two major areas of parent programs, infancy and preschool, are listed in terms of group training for mothers, home visiting programs, and guides for home stimulation activities.

EDRS Computer Microfilm
International Corporation
P. O. Box 190
Arlington, Virginia 22210 ($1.95 plus postage)

Kvaraceus, W. and Hayes, E. *If Your Child is Handicapped.* Boston: Porter Sargent, 1969.   **2**

A collection of personal statements intended for professionals, describing the experience of having a handicapped child. Includes eleven accounts by parents of cerebral palsied and orthopedically handicapped children, eight by parents of the mentally retarded, nine by parents of the deaf, six by parents of the emotionally disturbed, and seven by parents of children with special health problems.

Porter Sargent
11 Beacon Street
Boston, Massachusetts 02108 ($7.95)

Lane, M. B. "An Infant Center." *Children Today* 2 (May 1973): 22–24.   **6**

An interview with a teacher at the Oakland, California, Parent Child Center. Describes the Center's facility, programmatic operations, and type of parent participation.

U. S. Government Printing Office
Washington, D.C. 20402 ($1.25, issue)

Lane, M. B. *Education for Parenting.* Washington: National Association for the Education of Young Children, 1975.   **6**

The experiences of a director of nurseries in a cross-cultural education program, related to the broader needs of both parents and children. The book, which discusses the current status of parent education and provides alternatives for program development, is a useful planning guide for work with parents.

National Association for the Education of Young Children
1834 Connecticut Avenue, N.W.
Washington, D.C. 20009 ($3.00)

Larsen, L. and Bricker, W. *A Manual for Parents and Teachers of Severely and Moderately Retarded Children.* IMRID Papers and Reports, Volume 5, No. 22. Nashville, Tennessee: Peabody College, 1968.   **3, 5**

Sample activities designed to aid parents and teachers in changing the behavior of the mentally retarded child. Part I is oriented toward the methods and principles of behavior modification and examples of techniques are included. Part II is aimed at specifying in detail some of the activities to which these methods can be applied; some sample activities include: sitting quietly, playing with toys, various self-help skills, and talking in sentences. The appendices include: materials, reinforcers, sample forms for pre-test and post-test, and application to blind and deaf children.

IMRID Publications
George Peabody College
Box 154
Nashville, Tennessee 37203 ($2.00)

Lazar, J. and Chapman, J. *A Review of the Present Status and Future Research Needs of Programs to Develop Parenting Skills.* Washington: Social Research Group, George Washington University, 1972.   6

A state of the art paper which includes reviews of programs designed for parents. Abstracts of parent programs are categorized into three areas: parent-oriented, child-oriented, and omnibus (combination of approaches). Within each area, needs and gaps are identified, and a summary chapter provides an analysis of overall issues, needs and recommendations for further research.

Social Research Group
Suite 400
2401 Virginia Avenue, N.W.
Washington, D.C. 20037 (free)

Levenstein, P. "Cognitive Growth in Preschoolers Through Verbal Interaction With Mothers." *American Journal of Orthopsychiatry* 40 (1970): 426–432.   3

A brief description of the Mother-Child Home Program, its design, and some results after the first year of intervention. The article argues for a consideration of home-based programs by discussing how the verbal interaction project used home visitors as "toy demonstrators" to guide the mothers into greater verbalization and interaction with their children.

American Orthopsychiatric Association, Inc.
1790 Broadway
New York, New York 10019 ($4.50, issue)

Levenstein, P. "Learning Through (and From) Mothers." *Childhood Education* 48 (December 1971): 130–134.   2, 3, 5

A description of the Mother-Child Home Program which trains "Toy Demonstrators" to use verbal interaction techniques with mothers and their two-year-old children. The article emphasizes what the mothers have demonstrated to the program personnel and suggests the need for other programs to realize that demonstration is a "two-way" street.

Childhood Education
3615 Wisconsin Avenue, N.W.
Washington, D.C. 20402 ($1.75)

Lewis, M. and Rosenblum, L., eds. *The Effect of the Infant on Its Caregiver.*
New York: John Wiley and Sons, 1974.   **3, 5, 6**

A collection of recent research which looks at the child as a determinant of parental behavior, and a discussion of certain aspects of mother-child interaction which suggests major differences in existing home training approaches. With respect to preschool handicapped children, three especially relevant articles are: "Contributions of Human Infants to Caregiving and Social Interactions" by Richard Bell; "The Effect of the Infant's State, Level of Arousal, Sex and Ontogenetic Stage on the Caregiver" by Anneliese Korner; and a description of an intervention program for blind infants and their mothers by Selma Fraiberg.

John Wiley and Sons, Inc.
Eastern Distribution Center
1 Wiley Drive
Somerset, New Jersey 08873 ($14.95, Volume I)

Love, H. *Parental Attitudes Toward Exceptional Children.* Springfield, Illinois:
Charles C. Thomas, 1970.   **1**

A fairly basic collection of research on parental attitudes toward exceptionality in their children. While the major emphasis is on mental retardation, other exceptionalities—the gifted, blind, deaf, physically handicapped and emotionally disturbed—are discussed. A helpful overview is included which describes types of exceptionalities, incidence rates, and the assessment process.

Charles C. Thomas
301-327 East Lawrence Avenue
Springfield, Illinois 62717 ($9.50)

Mayer C. *Understanding Young Children,* 5 volumes. Urbana, Illinois: University of Illinois, 1974.   **1, 3, 5**

A set of books for teachers, parents and caregivers of "normal" and handicapped children. The five publications are available individually or as a set.

Publications Office
College of Education, University of Illinois
805 West Pennsylvania Avenue
Urbana, Illinois 61801 ($7.00, set; $1.25-$1.75 per publication)

McFadden, D., ed. *Early Childhood Development Programs and Services: Planning for Action.* Washington: National Association for the Education of Young Children, 1972.   6

The results of a conference on planning for the delivery of service to very young children. The book contains two excellent articles on parental involvement: (1) "Parent Involvement/Control in Child Development Programs," by Evelyn Moore and Maurine McKinley, discusses the need for greater community control of both services and research, and (2) "Parental Involvement: The Elixir of Change," by Jane Knitzer, looks at the rationale for parent involvement and argues that parents should have greater actual control and decision-making power.

National Association for the Education of Young Children
1834 Connecticut Avenue, N.W.
Washington, D.C. 20009 ($2.50)

Meadow, K. and Meadow, L. "Changing Role Perceptions for Parents of Handicapped Children." *Exceptional Children* 38 (September 1971): 21–27.   1

An examination of the socialization process of parents of handicapped children. The article discusses various aspects of the role to be learned, the part that professionals play as agents of parent socialization, and the effect of various factors (socio-economic status, age, etc.) on the transition in role perception.

Information Center
Council for Exceptional Children
1920 Association Drive
Reston, Virginia 22091 (free, one-copy journal)

A Mediated Training Program for Parents of Preschool or Mentally Retarded Children. Logan, Utah: Instructional Technology Project, Utah State University-Special Education, 1971.   3, 5

A mediated training package designed to equip parents of preschool mentally retarded children with the techniques necessary to train their children in self-help skills. The package contains four units; each unit has a participant's workbook and slide tape program. The units are: behavior (analysis of complex behaviors and the synthesis of simple behaviors into an instructional sequence), cues reinforcement, programming, and record keeping. A monitor's manual and script book are also included.

Instructional Technology Project
Utah State University
Exceptional Child Center, UMC-68
Logan, Utah 89322 ($200.00)

Moore, C., ed. *Preschool Programs for Handicapped Children.* Eugene, Oregon: Regional Resource Center for Handicapped Children, Center on Human Development, University of Oregon, 1974.   **5, 6**

A basic information package with suggestions on how to develop and operate preschool programs for handicapped children. It includes an excellent chapter on "Family Programs" which considers the following areas: selecting parent educators, scheduling, selecting program formats, parent involvement in preschool administration, and skill training for parents.

Northwest Regional Resource Center
Clinical Service Building, 3rd Floor
University of Oregon
Eugene, Oregon 97903 ($1.00)

Noland, R., ed. *Counseling Parents of the Mentally Retarded: A Sourcebook.* Springfield, Illinois: Charles C. Thomas, 1970.   **1**

A collection of articles dealing with aspects of parent counseling. The overview in the book deals with parental feelings and attitudes; part two deals with initial counseling needs for parents who have learned of their child's deficiency; part three discusses the group counseling process, for both orientation and therapeutic purposes; and other parts deal with parental and genetic counseling. The book's appendices list parents' associations, clinical programs, and audiovisual materials.

Charles C. Thomas
301-327 East Lawrence Avenue
Springfield, Illinois 62717 ($9.75)

Northcott, W. *Curriculum Guide: Hearing-Impaired Children—Birth to Three Years—and Their Parents.* St. Paul: Minnesota State Department of Education, 1971.   **3, 6**

A description of the components of a comprehensive infant program which focuses on a home-centered, parent-guided, natural language approach to learning based on the child's daily activities. The book provides guidelines for the development of the infant program, parent guidance and education, principles of language development, and parent-child interaction problems. Includes program objectives for parent and child and suggested daily home activities, as well as experience charts and auditory training exercises.

Minnesota State Department of Education
Department of Special Education
St. Paul, Minnesota 55101 ($6.50)

Northcott, W. "Language Development Through Parent Counseling and Guidance." *Volta Review* 68 (May 1966): 356–360.   **1, 2, 3**

A discussion of preschool education for the handicapped (deaf) through guidance with the parents. Considers such areas as parent needs, counselor qualifications, initial interview, additional visits, and language development. A method of language development is illustrated, and a rationale and specific goals for the child are offered.

Publications
3417 Volta Place, N.W.
Washington, D.C. 20007 ($ .50)

Northcott, W. "Parenting a Hearing-Impaired Child." *Hearing and Speech News* 41 (September-October 1973): 10–12, 28–29.   **6**

A description of a systems approach to parent participation in a program for ninety-six children under three years of age in the Minneapolis public schools. The program features information exchange, the facilitation of growth in parents through opportunities to practice child management, and the establishment of trust between parents and the teacher. Discusses various aids for parents, such as weekly visits, meetings for fathers only, mothers, and siblings.

NAHSA
814 Thayer Avenue
Silver Springs, Maryland 20910 ($ .20)

O'Dell, S. "Training Parents in Behavior Modification: A Review." *Psychological Bulletin* 81 (1974): 418–433.   **5**

A review of seventy articles on programs that employed behavior modification principles to assist parents in dealing with their children. Methods of producing behavior change in parents, the applicability of behavior modification in mental health, the historical development of such training, and technological issues involved in carrying out parent training programs are discussed.

American Psychological Association
1200 17th Street, N.W.
Washington, D.C. 20036 ($3.00, single issue)

Ora, J. P. *Home Programs.* Nashville: RIP Oppositional Child Technicians, George Peabody College, 1971.   **5**

Behavior modification programs to be used in the home by parents of oppositional children. Applies behavior-modification approach to potential problem areas: bathtime, bedtime, eating, yard, telephone, temper tantrums, and toilet training. Includes baseline instructions and step-by-step procedures. This program is appropriate for use in parent groups.

ERIC Document Reproduction Service
Leasco Information Products, Inc.
P.O. Drawer O
Bethesda, Maryland 20011 ($3.25 ERIC #ED070-220)

Ora, J. P. "Involvement and Training of Parent and Citizen Workers in Early Education for the Handicapped." *Not All Little Wagons are Red,* edited by M.B. Karnes. Reston, Virginia: Council for Exceptional Children, 1973.   **5, 6**

A description of the Tennessee Regional Intervention Program, which uses a few special educators as trainees and resource personnel for a program which is managed, implemented and evaluated by parents and citizen volunteers. Use of parents and citizen workers offers built-in consumer satisfaction, offers a partial solution to the manpower problem, and improves service.

Publication Sales
Council for Exceptional Children
1920 Association Drive
Reston, Virginia 22091 ($9.50)

Ora, J. P. "Parents and Citizen Workers." *Early Childhood Education and the Exceptional Child Cassette Album.* Reston, Virginia: Council for Exceptional Children, 1972.   **4, 6**

A twenty minute audio-tape which discusses citizen workers as early educators of the handicapped. Ora discusses citizen involvement in terms of examples of programs utilizing parents; why parent-implemented systems are important; citizen workers as a solution to the manpower crisis; and, the role of the professional as developer of automated instructional systems. The cost is $75.00 for complete set of five sixty-minute cassette tapes, made by thirteen professionals.

Publication Sales
Council for Exceptional Children
1920 Association Drive
Reston, Virginia 22091 ($75.00 set)

Page, R. "Co-parenting." *Children Today* 2 (May-June 1973): 21.   **6**

A mother's account of her year's experience at co-parenting, a situation in which two sets of parents share the care of a handicapped child. Both children, one autistic and the other brain-injured, are reported to have made gains. Co-parenting is suggested as an alternative to institutionalization.

U. S. Government Printing Office
Washington, D.C. 20402 ($1.25)

Park, C. "Searching for Help in Rearing and Educating a 'Special' Child: The Kind of Help Parents Need Most (and Least Often Get)." *Proceedings of a Workshop on the Needs of Young Children with Learning Disabilities.* Chapel Hill, North Carolina: University of North Carolina, 1968.   **6**

A mother's description of her search for help for her autistic child from professionals. The author describes the types of assistance parents would like to receive as they try to minimize the impact of the child's behavior on the families' activities.

Department of Special Education
Peabody Hall
University of North Carolina
Chapel Hill, North Carolina 27514 ($ .50)

Partners in Language—A Guide for Parents; Companeros en el Idioma—Gura para los Padres. Washington: American Speech and Hearing Association, 1973.   **3, 5**

A book concerned mainly with the normal language development of the young child, from birth to approximately three and one-half years of age. It was developed to increase parents' understanding and knowledge of early childhood language acquisition; and to provide useful suggestions to parents for developing communicative competence in young children by utilizing normal, daily activities as language learning experiences. Simplified developmental charts are included so that parents will be aware of some broad expectations in children's development. All materials are written in both Spanish and English in an easy-to-read format.

ASHA
9030 Old Georgetown Road
Washington, D.C. 20014 (free)

Patterson, G. R. and Gullion, M. E. *Living with Children: New Methods for Parents and Teachers.* Champaign, Illinois: Research Press, 1968.   **3, 5**

A detailed explanation of the manner in which the parent teaches the child and the child teaches the parent. The first section deals with how parents and children learn and it discusses reinforcers, accidental training, and retraining. The second section deals with changing undesirable behavior, such as in a child who fights too often; in an overly active child; or in a dependent, frightened, or withdrawn child.

Research Press
P. O. Box 3377
Country Fair Station
Champaign, Illinois ($3.50)

Perske, R. *New Directions for Parents of Persons Who are Retarded.* Nashville, Tennessee: Abingdon Press, 1973.   **2**

(Annotation by PCMR *Message*, January, 1974) For parents who elect to keep the retarded family member in their own home or a nearby residential facility. The book includes four sections which focus on "yourself, your child, the family, and society."

Abingdon Press
201 Eighth Avenue, S.
Nashville, Tennessee 37202 ($1.95)

The Portage Guide to Early Education. Portage, Wisconsin: Cooperative Educational Service, 1973.   **3, 5**

A developmentally formulated curriculum to be used with children, either handicapped or normal, between the mental ages of birth to five years. These materials can be used regardless of the specific handicapping condition(s), of the instructional delivery system (home, classroom, institution), of the teacher/child ratio, or of the professional status of the instructor. The Guide comes in two parts: a Checklist of Behaviors and a Card File containing curriculum ideas. These materials were developed and utilized by the Portage Project staff over a period of four years. Professional educators, paraprofessionals and parents have used these materials as a major source of behavioral evaluation and assessment and as a curriculum guide. The Checklist and Card File are color-coded and divided into five developmental areas: cognitive, self-help, motor, language, and socialization.

Cooperative Educational Service
Box 564
Portage, Wisconsin 53901 ($32.00 plus shipping)

Pushaw, D.; Collins, N.; Czuchna, G.; Gill, G.; O'Betts, G.; and Stahl, M. *Teach Your Child to Talk.* Cincinnati: CEBCO Standard Publishing Co., 1959.   **3, 5**

A training package designed to provide parents of preschool children with a better understanding of how they can help children learn to talk. The complete kit contains:

(1) Workshop manual (152 pages), with complete lesson plans for three workshops
(2) Two hundred 35mm color slides to augment the workshops
(3) A nineteen-minute cassette tape, recording examples of children's speech
(4) A 16mm color movie, which summarizes the major points made in the workshop
(5) A parent handbook which gives normal speech guidelines at appropriate age levels. Also included are suggested activities that parents can share with children and a suggested book list.
(6) A "Teach Me to Talk" booklet which is a cartoon booklet designed for parents of newborn children.

These materials would be useful with any group of parents that are interested in language development. The workshop is designed in such a way that it could be presented by most persons. The Parent Handbook is a useful resource and could be used separately.

Standard Publishing Company
8121 Hamilton Avenue
Cincinnati, Ohio 45231 ($275.00)

Quick, A., et al. *Enhancing Developmental Progress in Preschool Exceptional Children.* Memphis: Memphis State University, Department of Special Education and Rehabilitation, 1973.   **5, 6**

A description of the program components of Project Memphis which provides services to handicapped infants for the purpose of facilitating adoption and avoiding institutionalization. The book reviews programmatic aspects (administrative, financial, staff selection, and personnel training); recommends the development of individual programs for both children and parents; and describes procedures for planning such programs. Includes a bibliography of selected readings and the following appendices: a listing of educational equipment, suggestions for homemade equipment, and a listing of parent-assessment and child-assessment references.

Fearon Publishing Company
6 Davie Drive
Belmont, California 94002 ($4.00 retail; $3.00 school)

Radin, N. "Three Degrees of Maternal Involvement in a Preschool Program: Impact on Mothers and Children." *Child Development* 43 (December 1972): 1355–1364.   **6**

A study of seventy-one children in a preschool program who were separated into three matched groups: (1) no maternal involvement, (2) moderate maternal involvement, and (3) intense maternal involvement. At the end of the first year, no significant differences were found. One year later a follow-up study showed that the children in the two groups with maternal involvement made a significantly greater gain in Picture Vocabulary Test IQ than the children with no maternal involvement. The study strongly implies a need for follow-up data to assess the effects of maternal involvement.

University of Chicago Press
5801 South Ellis Avenue
Chicago, Illinois 60637 ($8.50, volume)

Roecker, V., et al. *Behavioral Prescription Guide. Manual II A: Communication.* Marshalltown, Iowa: The Marshalltown Project, 1973.   **3, 5**

Incremental behavioral objectives and strategies to aid parents in teaching handicapped infants and preschool children. This particular guide, which is intended for use in conjunction with group meetings and home visits, deals with development of communication skills.

Marshall-Powenshiek Joint County School System
Department of Special Education
9 Westwood Drive
Marshalltown, Iowa 50158 ($6.00)

Rotter, P. *A Parent's Program in a School for the Deaf.* Washington: Alexander Graham Bell Association for the Deaf, Inc., 1969.   **2, 6**

A monograph aimed at helping parents improve existing programs and improve their own efforts at raising a deaf child. Among the topics discussed are: the importance of parent involvement, the means of establishing school-home communication, the nature of parent programs, the role of parents and the schools in such programs, a mental health approach to meeting parents' needs, a survey of the types of parent activities, and the origin of parent education in the U.S. schools. Includes a list of sources to consult for help in strengthening parent programs.

Alexander Graham Bell Assoc. for the Deaf
Publication Sales
3417 Bolta Place, N.W.
Washington, D. C. 20007 ($6.00)

Rutter, M. *Maternal Deprivation Reassessed.* Baltimore: Penguin Books, Inc., 1972.   **6**

A review of theory and research on the short and long term effects of maternal deprivation in childhood. The rationale for environmental change before the child is three years of age is discussed and an argument for the term "maternal deprivation" being "reassessed" based on research evidence (to include such factors as stress and intra-familial relationships) is posed.

Penguin Books, Inc.
710 Ambassador Road
Baltimore, Maryland ($2.50)

Safran, D. "Making the Parents Feel at Home." *Day Care and Early Education*, Vol. 2. (March 1974): 11–14.   **6**

A discussion, by the director of the Center for the Study of Parent Involvement, of the misuses of parents in early childhood programs and suggestions of ways to change the situation. The author suggests that programs planning a parent involvement component must ask and answer each of the following questions: (1) Why involve parents?, (2) In what ways are parents being involved?, (3) What are parents doing and what is being done to them?, (4) How has parent involvement come about and how is it being maintained or thwarted?, (5) What impact is parent involvement having, and on whom?

Human Science Press
725 Fifth Avenue
New York, New York 10011 ($3.00, journal)

Schaefer, E. "Parents as Educators; Evidence from Cross-sectional, Longitudinal and Interventions Research." *The Young Child: Reviews of Research* Vol. 2, edited by W. W. Hartup. Washington: National Association for the Education of Young Children, 1972.   **5, 6**

A chapter on various conceptualizations of parent behaviors. The author reviews several views on the issue concerning which dimensions of parental behavior are of importance. This article is an excellent analysis of some of the evidence suggesting differential results from variations in parental behavior.

National Association for the Education of Young Children
1834 Connecticut Avenue, N.W.
Washington, D.C. 20009 ($5.75, volume)

Schilling, M. *Parent Participation in Infant Programs.* Technical Report #5 of A Nationally Organized Collaborative Project to Provide Comprehensive Services to Atypical Infants and Their Families. New York: United Cerebral Palsy Association, Inc., 1974.   **6**

Results of a questionnaire administered to ninety-six families for the purpose of exploring parental impressions and feelings toward the infant programs in which they were participating. The questionnaire dealt with six areas: (1) parents' first impression of the center, (2) parents' appraisal of the center beyond their first impression, (3) parents' plans for the immediate future of their child, (4) parents' concerns as to the child's present status and their desires for future program details, (5) parents' evaluation of their own role in the infant program, and (6) impact of the handicapped child and the program on family life style. Responses are included and conclusions/implications are offered. (A sequel is also available.)

UCP Collaborative (Infant) Project
66 East 34th Street
New York, New York 10016 ($1.00)

Schlesinger, H. and Meadow, K.P. *Sound and Sign: Childhood Deafness and Mental Health.* Berkeley: University of California Press, 1972.   **3, 6**

A theoretical framework, based on the work of Erik Erikson, for viewing the developmental problems associated with deafness. Research findings on the impact of deafness on mother-child interactions, on early language acquisition (spoken and manual), and on behavioral disorders are presented. A chapter on a comprehensive program of mental services for children and adults indicates that some of the developmental problems of deafness are amenable to change through early intervention.

University of California Press
2223 Fulton Street
Berkeley, California 94720 ($10.00)

Schopler, E. and Reichler, R. "Parents as Cotherapists in Treatment of Psychotic Children." *Journal of Autism and Childhood Schizophrenia* 1 (January-March 1971): 87–102.   **3, 5, 6**

A description of a treatment program for disturbed children in which parents are helped to function as change agents. Parents observe demonstrations of corrective approaches through a one-way screen. Parent participation includes program sessions and research activities at home.

Plenum Publications Corporation
227 West 17th Street
New York, New York 10011 ($10.00, journal)

Shearer, M. and Shearer, D. "The Portage Project: A Model for Early Childhood Education." *Exceptional Children* 39 (November 1972): 210–217.
          3, 5, 6

A report of a rural delivery system of home based intervention for multiply handicapped preschool children. A home teacher visited each parent and child once a week for one and one-half hours demonstrating an individualized curriculum. The parents then taught the curriculum and recorded resultant behavior. Results indicated that children progressed, and that parents can initiate, observe, and accurately record behavioral changes.

Information Center
Council for Exceptional Children
1920 Association Drive
Reston, Virginia 22091 (free, one copy)

Slavson, S. *Child-Centered Group Guidance of Parents.* New York: International University Press, 1958.   **3, 5, 6**

An extremely good source for a background on the group method of working with parents. The focus of this particular approach is one of sensitizing parents to the psychological needs of their children.

International University Press, Inc.
239 Park Avenue
New York, New York 10003 ($10.00)

Smith, L., et al. *Behavioral Prescription Guide. Manual II C: Social.* Marshalltown, Iowa: The Marshalltown Project, 1973.   **3, 5**

Incremental behavioral objectives and strategies to aid parents in teaching handicapped infants and preschool children. The guide is intended for use in conjunction with group meetings and home visits. This particular guide deals with development of social skills.

Marshall-Powenshiek Joint County Schools
Department of Special Education
9 Westwood Drive
Marshalltown, Iowa 50158 ($6.00)

Stakelon, A.E. *Early Childhood Newsletters: A Selected Guide.* Urbana, Illinois: University of Illinois, 1974.   **2**

A listing of newsletters and other serial publications concerned with topics of interest to educators and researchers working with young children.

Publications Office
College of Education, University of Illinois
805 West Pennsylvania Avenue
Urbana, Illinois 61801 ($ .75)

Stedman, D. *Current Issues in Mental Retardation and Human Development.* Washington: Department of Health, Education, and Welfare, Office of Mental Retardation Coordination, 1972.   **5, 6**

A collection of papers from a conference on mental retardation and families (1971). Among the topics are the following: family-support systems, a language-research/demonstration program in which parents are taught to train their children, the use of litigation for assessing needed services for retarded children, and the needs of the older handicapped citizen.

Office for Handicapped Individuals
Room 3517
OHEW Switzer Building
330 C Street, S.W.
Washington, D.C. 20201 (free, single copy)

Stein, M.; Beyer, E.; and Ronald, D. "Beyond Benevolence—The Mental Health Role of the Preschool Teacher," *Young Children* 30 (July 1975): 358-372.   **3, 5, 6**

A description of a four-year project in which teachers, under psychiatric supervision, have attempted to expand their functions with preschool children and their families. The methods that were used involved building relationships, sharing observations, and using the observations to help parents function more effectively in child-rearing.

Young Children
1834 Connecticut Avenue, N.W.
Washington, D.C. 20009 ($2.00, single issue)

Streissguth, A. and Bee, H. "Mother-Child Interactions and Cognitive Development in Children." *The Young Child: Reviews of Research* Vol. 2, edited by W.W. Hartup. Washington: National Association for the Education of Young Children, 1972.   **3, 5**

A very useful introduction to the title topic. Emphasis is on variations in maternal teaching strategies and the child's consequent intellectual development. Major methodological issues within mother/child research are discussed.

National Association for the Education of Young Children
1834 Connecticut Avenue, N.W.
Washington, D.C. 20009 ($5.75, volume)

Tavormina, J. "Basic Models of Parent Counseling: A Critical Review." *Psychological Bulletin* 81 (1974): 827–835.   **1, 4**

A definition of the structure and an evaluation of the research evidence on the effectiveness of two basic counseling models: the behavioral and the reflective. Includes analyses of design, methodology, and outcomes for each method. Both strategies have reported success. Exploration of the relative effectiveness of these models through comparative cost efficiency studies with specific problems and specific types of children is recommended by the author. The article offers a good source of references for parent counseling literature.

American Psychological Association
1200 17th Street, N.W.
Washington, D.C. 20036 ($3.00, issue)

Thomas, S.B., compiler. *Research on Approaches to Early Education: An Abstract Bibliography.* Urbana, Illinois: University of Illinois, 1974.   **6**

A list of documents and journal references covering family involvement, research on the long term effects of educational intervention programs, and research on specific program models.

Publications Office
College of Education, University of Illinois
805 West Pennsylvania Avenue
Urbana, Illinois 61801 ($2.00)

Understanding Young Children: Emotional and Behavioral Development and Disabilities. Urbana, Illinois: University of Illinois, 1974.   **2, 3, 5**

An example-filled booklet which emphasizes teaching techniques for helping young children gain emotional maturity and self-discipline.

Publications Office
College of Education, University of Illinois
805 West Pennsylvania Avenue
Urbana, Illinois 61801 ($1.75)

Understanding Your Children: The Handicapped Child in the Normal Preschool Class. Urbana, Illinois: University of Illinois, 1974.   **2, 3, 5**

Basic information concerning visual, auditory and motor disabilities, plus some suggestions for integrating the handicapped child into the normal classroom routines.

Publications Office
College of Education, University of Illinois
805 West Pennsylvania Avenue
Urbana, Illinois 61801 ($1.75)

Understanding Young Children: Intellectual Development and Intellectual Disabilities. Urbana, Illinois: University of Illinois, 1974.   **2, 3, 5**

A discussion of intellectual development and different stages of learning. Offers learning activity suggestions.

Publications Office
College of Education, University of Illinois
805 West Pennsylvania Avenue
Urbana, Illinois 61801 ($1.25)

Understanding Young Children: Language Development and Language Disabilities. Urbana, Illinois: University of Illinois, 1974.   **2, 3, 5**

An examination of factors involved in language development and the causes of language disabilities. Gives many suggestions for language activities.

Publications Office
College of Education, University of Illinois
805 West Pennsylvania Avenue
Urbana, Illinois 61801 ($1.25)

Understanding Young Children: Learning Development and Learning Disabilities. Urbana, Illinois: University of Illinois, 1974.   **2, 3, 5**

A discussion of heredity, maturation and environment. This booklet describes techniques to assist children in overcoming learning disabilities.

Publications Office
College of Education, University of Illinois
805 West Pennsylvania Avenue
Urbana, Illinois 61801 ($1.25)

Valenstein, T. *At Home with Children: A Resource Book for Family Day Care.* Urbana, Illinois: University of Illinois, 1975.   **6**

A collection of useful information, record-keeping suggestions, learning activities for young children, nutrition, health and safety tips, legal questions, etc. A description of the Educational Day Care Consultation Project at the University of Michigan is included.

Publications Office
College of Education, University of Illinois
805 West Pennsylvania Avenue
Urbana, Illinois 61801 ($3.50)

Walker, E. *Effective Observation for Educators.* Urbana, Illinois: University of Illinois, 1974.   **2, 3, 5**

An examination of the need for educators to be aware of how their own value systems can affect their interpretations of children's behavior.

Publications Office
College of Education, University of Illinois
805 West Pennsylvania Avenue
Urbana, Illinois 61801 ($ .50)

White, B. "An Analysis of Excellent Early Education Practices: Preliminary Report." *Interchange* 2 (1971): 71–88.   **3, 5**

A report on the first phase of the longitudinal Harvard Preschool Project which is designed to yield information on how to raise children to develop optimally during the first six years of life. Findings to date suggest that effective mothers (1) are generally permissive, (2) usually but not always respond to their child's appeals for immediate help, (3) act in response to the child, and (4) have a high energy level. Developmental divergence among children appears at the time when the child develops increased motor and verbal ability.

Interchange
252 Bloom Street West
Toronto 5, Ontario
Canada ($3.00 issue)

White, B. and Watts, J. *Experience and Environment: Major Influences on the Development of the Young Child,* Vol. 1. Englewood Cliffs, New Jersey: Prentice-Hall, Inc., 1973.   **3, 5, 6**

A longitudinal study, based on data from the Harvard Preschool Project, of child development as related to effective and ineffective child-rearing techniques. Contrasts experiences of the A children (above average competence) and the C children (below average competence). Results point to a critical period of development, from ten to eighteen months of age, in which child-rearing patterns tend to have their strongest effects.

Prentice-Hall, Inc.
Englewood Cliffs, New Jersey 07632 ($14.95)

Williams, D. and Jaffa, E. *Ice Cream, Poker Chips, and Very-Goods: A Behavior Modification Manual for Parents.* College Park, Maryland: The Maryland Book Exchange, 1971.   **2, 3, 5**

A manual to teach parents the basic concepts and language of behavior modification; to train parents in the practical application of these techniques with their own children; and to increase the frequency of the parents' use of these techniques within the home. The basic content of the manual is directly derived from the research literature on the functional analysis of behavior. It covers reinforcers, changing behavior, and maintaining changes.

The Maryland Book Exchange
4500 College Avenue
College Park, Maryland 20740 ($2.75)

Wilson, G. and Pavloff, G. *Adult Involvement in Child Development for Staff and Parents.* Atlanta: Humanics Press, 1972.   **4, 5, 6**

A fairly simple booklet offering step-by-step techniques for parent involvement. This publication discusses solutions for common problems in parent involvement and provides training exercises for parents and staff. It also includes information on the use of parents as policymakers.

Humanics Associate
881 Peachtree Street, N.E.
Atlanta, Georgia 30309 ($6.00)

Index

Note: Page references in **boldface** refer to figures.